LET THE BIBLE TEACH YOU CHRISTIAN DOCTRINE

Let the Bible teach you Christian Doctrine

John Jefferson Davis

THE PATERNOSTER PRESS
EXETER

AUSTRALIA:
Bookhouse Australia Ltd.,
P.O. Box 115, Flemington Markets, NSW 2129

SOUTH AFRICA:
Oxford University Press,
P.O. Box 1141, Cape Town

British Library Cataloguing in Publication Data

Davis, John J.
Let the bible teach you Christian doctrine.
I. Title
220.5′2 BS391.2

ISBN 0-85364-407-1

Photoset in Great Britain by
Photoprint, 9–11 Alexandra Lane, Torquay, Devon
and printed for The Paternoster Press,
Paternoster House, 3 Mount Radford Crescent, Exeter, Devon
by A. Wheaton & Co. Ltd., Exeter, Devon.

Dedication

To my students at Gordon-Conwell Theological Seminary

CONTENTS

Preface 11

1. Scripture 13
Verbal Inspiration 13
Inerrancy 17

2. God 19
Existence 19
Divine Attributes: Perfections of the Divine Nature 21
Metaphysical Attributes 21
1. Independence 21
2. Spirituality 22
3. Immutability 22
4. Eternity 23
5. Simplicity 23
6. Omnipresence 23
7. Omnipotence 24
8. Omniscience 25
Moral Attributes 26
1. Holiness 26
2. Love 26
3. Wisdom 27
4. Grace and Mercy 28
5. Goodness 29
6. Patience 29
7. Righteousness and Justice 30
8. Truthfulness 31
9. Faithfulness 32
Trinity 33
1. Personality of the Spirit 33
2. Deity of the Spirit 34
3. General Texts 35
Election 35
1. Arminian View 35
2. Calvinistic View 37

3. **Creation** 41

4. **Providence** 43
Nature 43
World History 44
Personal Circumstances 45

5. **Man** 47
Man's Original State 47
Aspects of Human Nature 48
Trichotomy 49
Dichotomy 49
Man in the State of Sin 49
Original Sin 49
Personal Sin 50
Manifestations and Consequences of Sin 51

6. **Person of Christ** 55
Preexistence 55
Virgin Birth 56
Sinlessness 58
Humanity 59
Deity 61
Divine Titles 61
1. "Mighty God" 61
2. "Son of God" in a Unique Sense 62
Divine Attributes or Qualities 62
1. Eternity, Preexistence 62
2. Not Limited by Space 63
3. Universal Power and Authority 63
4. Has Life in Himself 63
Divine Actions and Prerogatives 63
1. Active in Creation of the World 63
2. Sustains the Universe 63
3. Authority to Forgive Sins 64
4. Object of Prayer 64
5. Object of Worship 64
6. Power to Raise the Dead 64
7. Final Judge of Mankind 64
New Testament Texts on Equality or Identity of Christ and God 65
1. Equality 65
2. Identity 65

7. Work of Christ 67
Preaching, Teaching, Miracles 67
Obedience of Christ 69
Death on the Cross 70
Resurrection and Ascension 72

8. Salvation and the Christian Life 75
Calling and Regeneration 75
Repentance and Faith 77
Justification 79
Sanctification 81
Wesleyan View 81
Reformed View 82
Pentecostal Distinctives 83
Perseverance 86
Reformed View 86
Wesleyan/Arminian View 87

9. The Church 91
Nature of the Church 91
Biblical Names and Descriptions 91
Attributes of the Church 93
Government of the Church 95
General Texts 95
1. Congregational Church Government 97
2. Presbyterian Church Government 98
3. Episcopal Church Government 99
Mission of the Church 100

10. Sacraments 105
Baptism 105
General Texts 105
Believer's Baptism 106
Infant Baptism 107
Lord's Supper 109
General Texts 109
Lutheran View 111
Reformed and Wesleyan Views 111
Zwinglian View 112

11. Individual Eschatology 115
Death 115
Intermediate State 117

12. General Eschatology 121
The Second Coming of Christ 121
Millennial Views 124
Premillennial, Pretribulational 125
Premillennial, Posttribulational 126
Amillennial 127
Postmillennial 127
The General Resurrection 129
The Final Judgment 131
The Eternal State 134

PREFACE

This small volume grows out of a desire to assist seminary and college students in their study of Christian theology. There is great value in looking up the Scripture references on a given topic listed in a textbook, but often time pressure and inertia conspire against such good intentions on the reader's part. By listing important Scripture references in the order in which they are usually presented in standard systematic theologies, I hope to both save the reader time in this connection and keep the study of theology grounded in the actual text of Scripture.

This volume could also be used as a convenient survey of Bible doctrine for adult Sunday school classes, or for personal devotional reading. Many of the Scripture texts have explanatory annotations, and suggestions for further study are given for each topic.

I would like to extend a special word of thanks to Bill and Lisanne Bales who assisted in the research, and to Carrie Powell, who very patiently typed the manuscript.

John Jefferson Davis
South Hamilton, Massachusetts

FOR FURTHER READING

Each chapter ends with a bibliography, compiled by Brian Butler, of Moorlands College, from the many books available. He writes: "We have tried to give titles from several levels of treatment. The letters (A), (B), and (C) after each title may be read as follows:

(A) Basic but none the worse for that
(B) More advanced—and probably more demanding
(C) Fairly technical

We have restricted publication details to the date and the number of pages. Where possible the first date of publication is given. The number of pages in a book is usually a fair guide to the size of treatment."

1

SCRIPTURE

Historic Christianity has from the beginning acknowledged the Bible to be the highest authority for faith and practice. Evangelical Christians believe in the *verbal inspiration* and *inerrancy* of Scripture: the very words of the original texts, and not merely the general concepts or ideas, were inspired by God, and hence are free from error in their teachings.

"We must make a great difference between God's Word and the word of man. A man's word is a little sound, that flies into the air, and soon vanishes; but the Word of God is greater than heaven and earth . . . for it forms part of the power of God, and endures everlastingly; we should, therefore, diligently study God's Word, and know and assuredly believe that God himself speaks unto us" (Martin Luther, *Table Talk,* XLIV).

Verbal Inspiration

Ex 4:12–16 "Now go; I [God] will help you [Moses] speak and will teach you what to say." But Moses said, "O Lord, please send someone else to do it." Then the Lord's anger burned against Moses and he said, "What about your brother, Aaron the Levite? . . . You shall speak to him and put words in his mouth; I will help both of you speak and will teach you what to do. He will speak to the people for you, and it will be as if he were your mouth and as if you were God to him."[1]

Ex 17:14 Then the Lord said to Moses, "Write this on a scroll as something to be

[1]As Moses puts specific words in Aaron's mouth, so God puts specific words in Moses' mouth. The relationship could be represented as follows: God: Moses::Moses:Aaron.

remembered and make sure that Joshua hears it, because I will completely erase the memory of the Amalekites from under heaven."[2]

Ex 20:1 And God spoke all these words. . . .

Ex 31:18 When the Lord finished speaking to Moses on Mount Sinai, he gave him the two tablets of the Testimony, the tablets of stone inscribed by the finger of God.

Ex 34:27 Then the Lord said to Moses, "Write down these words, for in accordance with these words I have made a covenant with you and with Israel."[3]

Nu 22:38 Balaam replied. ". . . I must speak only what God puts in my mouth."

Nu 23:5 The Lord put a message in Balaam's mouth and said, "Go back to Balak and give him this message."

Nu 24:12–13 Balaam answered Balak, "Did I not tell the messengers you sent me, 'Even if Balak gave me his palace filled with silver and gold, I could not do anything of my own accord, good or bad, to go beyond the command of the Lord—and I must say only what the Lord says'?"

Nu 24:15–16 "The oracle of Balaam son of Beor . . . the oracle of one who hears the words of God."[4]

Nu 33:2 [Israel's wilderness journey]: At the Lord's command Moses recorded the stages in their journey.[5]

Dt 18:18 "I [God] will raise up for them [Israelites] a prophet like you [Moses] from among their brothers; I will put my words in his mouth, and he will tell them everything I command him."[6]

Isa 8:1 The Lord said to me, "Take a large scroll and write on it with an ordinary pen: Maher-Shalal-Hash-Baz."[7]

Isa 30:8–9 Go now, write it on a tablet for them, inscribe it on a scroll, that for the days to come it may be an everlasting witness. These are rebellious people . . . children

[2]"This" refers to the specific words of the account in Ex 17:8–16 of Israel's victory over the Amalekites.

[3]"These words" have reference to the two tablets mentioned in 34:1 and the specific commandments cited in this chapter.

[4]Even though the NT mentions Balaam in an unfavourable light (Jude 11: "they [false teachers] have rushed for profit into Balaam's error"), his commission to speak illustrates the nature of true prophecy. The messenger is sent to speak God's words, not his own.

[5]Note here the explicit claim to Mosaic authorship of this section of the Book of Numbers.

[6]Again, notice the nature of true prophecy: *I will put my words in his mouth.* This prophecy was fulfilled in the succession of Old Testament prophets after Moses, and preemeninently in Jesus Christ. Cf. Jn 7:16, "Jesus answered, 'My teaching is not my own. It comes from him who sent me.' "

[7]God commands Isaiah to give his son a specific name which means "Quick to the plunder, swift to the spoil," referring to the foreign invaders (e.g. Egypt and Assyria, 7:18) who will be God's instruments of judgment upon a rebellious Israel.

unwilling to listen to the Lord's instruction.

Jer 1:9 Then the Lord reached out his hand and touched my mouth and said to me, "Now, I have put my words in your mouth."

Jer 5:14 Therefore this is what the Lord God Almighty says: "Because the people have spoken these words, I will make my words in your mouth a fire and these people the wood it consumes."

Jer 25:13 I [God] will bring upon that land all the things I have spoken against it, all that are written in this book and prophesied by Jeremiah against all the nations.

Jer 30:1–2 This is the word that came to Jeremiah from the Lord: "This is what the Lord, the God of Israel, says: 'Write in a book all the words I have spoken to you.' "

Eze 24:1 In the ninth year, in the tenth month on the tenth day, the word of the Lord came to me.[8]

Hab 2:2 Then the Lord replied: "Write down the revelation and make it plain on tablets so that a herald may run with it."

Mt 4:4 Jesus answered, "It is written: 'Man does not live on bread alone, but on every word that comes from the mouth of God.' "[9]

Mt 22:41–44 While the Pharisees were gathered together, Jesus asked them, "What do you think about the Christ? Whose son is he?" "The son of David," they replied. He said to them, "How is it then that David, speaking by the Spirit, calls him 'Lord'? For he says, " 'The Lord said to my Lord: "Sit at my right hand until I put your enemies under your feet." ' "[10]

Jn 14:26 "But the Counsellor, the Holy Spirit, whom the Father will send in my name, will teach you all things and will remind you of everything I have said to you."[11]

Jn 15:26 "When the Counsellor comes, whom I will send to you from the Father, the Spirit of truth who goes out from the Father, he will testify about me."

[8]These and similar expressions are common in Ezekiel and the other OT prophets. Cf. Eze 26:1, 27:1, 28:1, 29:1, 30:1, 32:1, 33:1, 34:1, 35:1, 36:1, 38:1.

[9]For Jesus, the entire OT came from the mouth of God. See John Wenham, *Christ and the Bible,* pp. 11–37.

[10]The quotation is from Ps 110:1. Notice that even though the text of Ps 110 makes no *explicit* reference to the Spirit's inspiration, according to the Lord Jesus, David *spoke by the Spirit.*

[11]Jesus promises the disciples the supernatural assistance of the Holy Spirit for their teaching ministry.

Jn 16:12–15 "I have much more to say to you, more than you can now bear. But when he, the Spirit of truth, comes, he will guide you into all truth. . . . the Spirit will take from what is mine and make it known to you."

Ac 4:25 "You [God] spoke by the Holy Spirit through the mouth of your servant, our Father David: 'Why do the nations rage, and the peoples plot in vain?' "[12]

Ro 3:1–2 What advantage, then, is there in being a Jew, or what value is there in circumcision? Much in every way! First of all, they have been entrusted with the very words of God.[13]

1Co 2:13 This is what we speak, not in words taught us by human wisdom but in words taught by the Spirit, expressing spiritual truths in spiritual words.

1Co 14:37 If anybody thinks he is a prophet or spiritually gifted, let him acknowledge that what I [Paul] am writing to you is the Lord's command.[14]

2Co 13:2–3 On my return I will not spare those who sinned earlier or any of the others, since you are demanding proof that Christ is speaking through me.[15]

1Th 2:13 And we also thank God continually because, when you received the word of God, which you heard from us, you accepted it not as the word of men, but as it actually is, the word of God, which is at work in you who believe.

**2Ti 3:16–17* All Scripture is God-breathed and is useful for teaching, rebuking, correcting and training in righteousness, so that the man of God may be thoroughly equipped for every good work.[16]

Heb 3:7–8 So, as the Holy Spirit says: "Today, if you hear his voice, do not harden your hearts. . . ."[17]

**2Pe 1:20–21* Above all, you must understand that no prophecy of Scripture came about by the prophet's own interpretation. For prophecy never had its origin in the will

[12]According to Peter and John, the words of Ps 2 are the words of the Holy Spirit, and not merely those of David, the human author.

[13]According to the apostle Paul, the OT canon represents the very words of God (or, "oracles": *ta logia tou Theou).* An oracle is the direct speech of a deity to man. See Warfield, "The Oracles of God," in *The Inspiration and Authority of the Bible,* pp. 351–407.

[14]In chapter 7 of this letter Paul does couch some of his teaching in the form of advice, but the epistle as a whole—as 14:37 makes clear—bears the stamp of Christ's divine authority.

[15]By reminding the contentious members of the Corinthian church that Christ was *speaking through him,* Paul was placing his ministry on the same level as that of the OT prophets: a specially commissioned spokesman for God.

[16]"All Scripture is God-breathed" *(pāsa graphē theopneustos):* like Adam himself, the Scripture is said to be the immediate creation of the divine Spirit/breath. Another possible translation, "Every scripture inspired by God is profitable . . ." does not remove the force of this classic text, since, for the NT writers, the entire OT canon was Scripture, and hence divinely inspired. See Warfield, "God-Inspired Scripture," in *The Inspiration and Authority of the Bible,* pp. 245–96.

[17]A quotation from Ps 95. As do the other NT writers, the author of Hebrews assigns the Psalter and the OT in its entirety to the work of the Holy Spirit.

of man, but men spoke from God as they were carried along by the Holy Spirit.[18]

2Pe 3:16 His letters contain some things that are hard to understand, which ignorant and unstable people distort, as they do other Scriptures, to their own destruction.[19]

Inerrancy[20]

Ps 12:6 And the words of the Lord are flawless, like silver refined in a furnace of clay, purified seven times.

Ps 18:30 As for God, his way is perfect; the word of the Lord is flawless.[21]

Ps 19:7 The law of the Lord is perfect, reviving the soul.

Ps 19:9 The ordinances of the Lord are sure and altogether righteous.

Ps 119:89 Your word, O Lord is eternal; it stands firm in the heavens.[22]

Ps 119:151 Yet you are near, O Lord, and all your commands are true.

Ps 119:160 All your words are true; all your righteous laws are eternal.

Ps 119:172 May my tongue sing of your word, for all your commands are righteous.

Pr 30:5–6 "Every word of God is flawless; he is a shield to those who take refuge in him. Do not add to his words or he will rebuke you and prove you a liar."

Mt 4:4 Jesus answered, "It is written: 'Man does not live on bread alone, but on every word that comes from the mouth of God.' "[23]

Lk 24:25 He [Jesus] said to them [disciples on Emmaus road], "How foolish you are, and how slow of heart to believe all that the prophets have spoken!"

**Jn 10:35* ". . . the Scripture cannot be broken."[24]

Jn 17:17 "Sanctify them by the truth; your word is truth."

[18]A clear statement about the supernatural origin of Scripture. Note that in the NT view, the entire OT canon was *prophetic* in nature, not just the prophets *per se*. David was a *prophet,* according to Peter (Ac 2:30), knowing full well that his words were recorded in the Psalms. The word in v. 21 translated as "carried along" *(pheromenoi)* is also found in Ac 27:15, referring to the strong wind driving the boat carrying Paul to Rome. In 2 Peter, the word suggests the strong influence of the Spirit coming upon the biblical writer from without.

[19]Already within the NT period the Pauline epistles are being classed with the *other Scriptures (tas loipas graphas).*

[20]All the texts cited in this section in relation to *verbal inspiration* are directly relevant to *inerrancy.* All Scripture is the direct product of the omnipotent and omniscient God who is not subject to error.

[21]The word translated here as "flawless" is a participial form of the verb *tsaraph,* used in reference to purging gold or silver by fire, and to separate from dross, Ps 12:6[7], Isa 1:25. The implication is that God's word is free from all dross and impurities.

[22]Cf. the words of Christ in Mt 24:35: "Heaven and earth will pass away, but my words will never pass away." The word of God is more enduring than the physical universe itself.

[23]For Jesus and the NT writers, the entire canonical OT came from the mouth of God.

[24]*ou dunatai luthēai hē graphē:* from *luō;* here,

Ac 24:14 "I [Paul] believe everything that agrees with the Law and that is written in the Prophets."[25]

"annul, subvert, do away with, deprive of authority" (Thayer, *Greek-English Lexicon of the NT).* Notice how Christ here defends his claim to equality with God (10:30) by appealing to a *single word* (*theoi,* gods) from a non-Davidic psalm, Ps 82:6—thus demonstrating his sublime confidence in the unshakable authority of Scripture.

[25] "The Law and the prophets" was a term used to designate the OT as a whole: cf. Mt 5:17, "Do not think that I have come to abolish the Law or the Prophets; I have not come to abolish them but to fulfil them."

FOR FURTHER READING

Scripture

"The authority of scripture", art. by G. W. Bromiley in *New Bible Commentary Revised* (1970), pp.3–11. (A)
"Revelation and inspiration", art. by J. I. Packer, in *New Bible Commentary Revised,* pp.12–18. (A)
PACKER, J. I. *God has spoken* (1965), 93pp. (A)
WENHAM, J. W. *Christ and the Bible* (1972), 206pp. (B)
HORN, R. M. *The Book that speaks for itself* (1969), 127pp. (A)
Scripture and Truth, ed. D. A. Carson and J. D. Woodbridge (1983), 446pp. (B)
WARFIELD, B. B. *The authority and inspiration of the Bible,* 442pp. (C)

2

GOD

"True and substantial wisdom principally consists of two parts, the knowledge of God, and the knowledge of ourselves" (John Calvin, *Institutes,* I.1.1).

The Scripture texts in this section relate to four main areas: God's existence, divine attributes or perfections, triune nature, and eternal decrees concerning man and world history. The doctrine of God is foundational for all aspects of Christian theology, and is central in both the Old and New Testaments.

Existence

Ge 1:1 In the beginning God created the heavens and the earth.[1]

Ps 14:1 The fool says in his heart, "There is no God."[2]

Ps 19:1 The heavens declare the glory of God; the skies proclaim the work of his hands.[3]

Ac 14:17 "Yet he has not left himself without testimony: He has shown kindness by giving you rain from heaven and crops in their seasons; he provides you with plenty of food and fills your hearts with joy."[4]

Ac 17:24–28 "The God who made the world and everything in it is the Lord of heaven and earth and does not live in temples built by hands. And he is not served by human hands, as if he needed anything, because he himself gives all men life and breath and

[1]The Bible nowhere attempts to give a philosophical proof of God's existence. From the very beginning of biblical revelation, as here in Ge 1:1, it is always presupposed.

[2]Here, as elsewhere in Scripture, "fool" is more a moral than merely intellectual category. Only moral and spiritual obtuseness can lead one to deny God's reality. The atheism spoken of here in 14:1 is more likely a "practical" rather than merely theoretical atheism, in that the fool ignores the implications of God's existence for his own life.

[3]God's existence, power, and glory are evidenced in the wonders of creation (cf. Ro 1:19–20). Theologians

everything else. From one man he made every nation of men, that they should inhabit the whole earth; and he determined the times set for them and the exact places where they should live. God did this so that men would seek him and perhaps reach out for him and find him, though he is not far from each one of us. 'For in him we live and move and have our being.' As some of your own poets have said, 'We are his offspring.' "[5]

**Ro 1:18–20* The wrath of God is being revealed from heaven against all the godlessness and wickedness of men who suppress the truth by their wickedness, since what may be known about God is plain to them, because God has made it plain to them. For since the creation of the world God's invisible qualities—his eternal power and divine nature—have been clearly seen, being understood from what has been made, so that men are without excuse.[6]

Ro 2:14–15 Indeed, when Gentiles, who do not have the law, do by nature things required by the law, they are a law for themselves, even though they do not have the law, since they show that the requirements of the law are written on their hearts, their consciences also bearing witness, and their thoughts now accusing, now even defending them.[7]

Heb 11:6 And without faith it is impossible to please God, because anyone who comes to him must believe that he exists and that he rewards those who earnestly seek him.[8]

refer to this as "general revelation," in contrast to the "special revelation" found in the Scriptures.

[4]The words of Paul and Barnabas to the crowds in Lystra and Derbe. The regularities of nature point not only to God's existence, but to his goodness and benevolence as well.

[5]Paul's evangelistic speech at the Areopagus in Athens. The citation of the pagan poets Epimenides and Aratus shows that, in Paul's view, they had an awareness of God's existence.

[6]One of the most important scriptural texts on the knowability and existence of God. The evidence of creation is so clear, Paul says, that the unbeliever is morally *without excuse.* The term in v. 18 *(katechein)* translated as "suppress" here has the negative connotation of "holding illegally" or "holding in prison." See R. C. Sproul, *The Psychology of Atheism,* pp. 57–63. "Paul's complaint is not that men failed to know God, but that they failed to honor Him. Herein is the universal indictment of man" (63).

[7]According to the apostle Paul, the natural man has an awareness of God not only through the creation, but also through the moral law written upon the conscience.

[8]The faith in question here involves no mere intellectual assent to God's existence as such, but a positive disposition of the heart toward God as a benevolent rewarder of the sincere seeker.

Divine Attributes: Perfections of the Divine Nature

"This one, eternal, omnipresent Being is likewise all-perfect. He has, from eternity to eternity, all the perfections and infinitely more than it ever did or ever can enter into the heart of man to conceive; yea, infinitely more than the angels in heaven can conceive: These perfections we usually term, the attributes of God" (John Wesley, Sermon, "The Unity of The Divine Being").

METAPHYSICAL ATTRIBUTES

Those implying an absolute distinction between God and man.

1. *Independence*

Self-existence or aseity; God's being is grounded only in himself; God's being is in no way dependent on the creature.

Is 40:13–14 Who has understood the Spirit of the Lord, or instructed him as his counsellor? Whom did the Lord consult to enlighten him, and who taught him the right way? Who was it that taught him knowledge or showed him the path of understanding?

Is 44:24 "I am the Lord, who has made all things, who alone stretched out the heavens, who spread out the earth by myself."

Jn 5:26 "For as the Father has life in himself, so he has granted the Son to have life in himself."[9]

Ac 17:25 "And he [God] is not served by human hands, as if he needed anything, because he himself gives all men life and breath and everything else."[10]

Ro 11:34–35 "Who has known the mind of the Lord? Or who has been his counsellor? Who has ever given to God, that God should repay him?"[11]

Rev 4:11 "You are worthy, our Lord and God, to receive glory and honour and power, for you created all things, and by your will they were created and have their being."[12]

[9]God, who is the source of all life, alone has *life in himself.* The theory of evolution attributes to the impersonal forces of matter, time, and chance the life-originating power that the Scriptures attribute to God.

[10]God's independence, and man's *dependence,* imply that man has no cause for pride or boasting. In both his natural existence and in his salvation man's fundamental relationship to God is that of dependence.

[11]The apostle Paul here quotes from Isa 40:13 and Job 41:11.

[12]In every breath, in every heartbeat, we are dependent upon God for our very life and being. This realization leads not only to humility on the part of the creature, but rightfully is a cause of praise and worship to the Creator.

2. *Spirituality*

God is pure spirit, having no bodily or material parts,[13] and invisible to the physical eye.

Ex 20:4 "You shall not make for yourself an idol in the form of anything in the heaven above or on the earth beneath or in the waters below."[14]

Jn 4:24 "God is spirit, and his worshippers must worship in spirit and in truth."

1Ti 1:17 Now to the King eternal, immortal, invisible, the only God, be honour and glory for ever and ever. Amen.

1Ti 6:15–16 . . . God, the blessed and only Ruler, the King of kings and Lord of lords, who alone is immortal and who lives in unapproachable light, whom no one has seen or can see.

3. *Immutability*

God is unchanging in the perfection of his character, nature, purposes, and promises.[15]

Nu 23:19 "God is not a man, that he should lie, nor a son of man, that he should change his mind."

Ps 33:11 But the plans of the Lord stand firm forever, the purposes of his heart through all generations.

Ps 102:27 But you [God] do not change, and your years will never end. *Mal 3:6*: I the Lord do not change. So you, O descendants of Jacob, are not destroyed.[16]

Heb 6:17 Because God wanted to make the unchanging nature of his purpose very clear to the heirs of what was promised, he confirmed it with an oath.[17]

**Jas 1:17* Every good and perfect gift is from above, coming down from the Father of the heavenly lights, who does not change like shifting shadows.

[13]Some cults, such as the Mormons, falsely ascribe a physical nature to God. Biblical expressions such as God's "right hand" and the like are figurative expressions for aspects of God's relationship to man. The Bible makes use of expressions drawn from common human experience to describe intangible and invisible spiritual realities.

[14]God's spirituality, and hence invisibility, is the presupposition behind the second commandment.

[15]Immutability does not imply lack of movement or activity on God's part; the God of Scripture is the God of dynamic life. The language of God's "repentance" (e.g., Ex 32:14) indicates a change in man's relationship to God, not a change in God's character or ultimate purpose for man. "Repentance" by God can also refer to God's *self-restraint* and *patience* in the face of disobedience on the part of his people: "Return to the Lord, your God, for he is gracious and merciful, slow to anger, and abounding in steadfast love, and repents of evil" (Joel 2:13, RSV: "He relents from sending calamity," NIV). God's immutability and unwavering purpose is the ultimate ground for our personal *assurance of salvation.*

[16]Israel did not receive the *immediate* judgment it deserved because of God's mercy and the covenant made with Abraham, Isaac, and Jacob. Cf. Ge 17:7, "I will establish my covenant as an everlasting covenant between me and you and your descendants after you for the generations to come, to be your God and the God of your descendants after you."

4. *Eternity*

God is not a created being and is not subject to the limitations of time.

**Dt 33:27* "The eternal God is your refuge, and underneath are the everlasting arms."[18]

Ps 90:2 Before the mountains were born or you brought forth the earth and the world, from everlasting to everlasting you are God.

Ps 102:12, 27 But you, O Lord, sit enthroned forever, your renown endures through all generations . . . you remain the same and your years will never end.[19]

Isa 57:15 For this is what the high and lofty One says—he who lives forever, whose name is holy: "I live in a high and holy place, but also with him who is contrite and lowly in spirit."[20]

**1Ti 1:17* Now to the King eternal, immortal, invisible, the only God, be honour and glory for ever and ever. Amen.

[17]Referring to God's oath of ratification of the covenant with Abraham: Heb 6:13, "When God made his promise to Abraham, since there was no one greater for him to swear by, he swore by himself'; Ge 22:17, "I will surely bless you and make your descendants as numerous as the stars in the sky and as the sand on the seashore."

[18]God's eternity implies that his ability to care for us can never end.

[19]The shortness and transience of man's life are contrasted with God's eternity.

[20]"For thus says the high and lofty One who inhabits eternity" (RSV).

5. *Simplicity*

God is one in essence; there are no divisions or contrary elements within his nature. The simplicity and integrity of the divine nature are presupposed, though not explicitly stated, in texts such as the following:

Dt 6:4 Hear, O Israel: the Lord our God, the Lord is one.[21]

2Co 1:19 For the Son of God, Jesus Christ, who was preached among you by me and Silas and Timothy, was not "Yes" and "No," but in him it has always been "Yes."[22]

[21]God is one both *quantitatively* (there is only one true God) and *qualitatively* (one united, self-consistent, and perfectly integrated nature). The three persons of the Trinity—Father, Son, and Holy Spirit represent *distinctions* within the divine nature, but not *division* or *separation.*

[22]The consistency of Paul's gospel reflects the consistency of the life and character of Jesus Christ, who himself manifests the inner consistency of God's own nature.

6. *Omnipresence*

God is not limited or bounded by space, yet is present throughout all space.

1Ki 8:27 "But will God really dwell on earth? The heavens, even the highest heaven, cannot contain you. How much less this temple I have built!"[23]

[23]Solomon's prayer at the dedication of the Temple.

Ps 139:7–10 Where can I go from your Spirit? Where can I flee from your presence? If I go up to the heavens, you are there; if I make my bed in the depths, you are there. If I rise on the wings of the dawn, if I settle on the far side of the sea, even there your hand will guide me, your right hand will hold me fast.[24]

Jer 23:23–24 "Am I only a God nearby," declares the Lord, "and not a God far away? Can anyone hide in secret places so that I cannot see him?" declares the Lord. "Do not I fill heaven and earth?" declares the Lord.[25]

Ac 17:27–28 "God did this [created man; providentially supervised the course of his life] so that men would seek him and perhaps reach out for him and find him, though he is not far from each one of us. 'For in him we live and move and have our being.' "[26]

7. *Omnipotence*

God can do all things consistent with his holy nature and will; nothing can frustrate the accomplishment of his sovereign purpose.[27]

Ge 18:14 "Is anything too hard for the Lord? I will return to you at the appointed time next year and Sarah will have a son."[28]

2Ch 20:6 "O Lord, God of our Fathers, are you not the God who is in heaven? You rule over all the kingdoms of the nations. Power and might are in your hand, and no one can withstand you."[29]

Ps 147:5 Great is our Lord and mighty in power; his understanding has no limit.

Isa 14:27 For the Lord Almighty has purposed, and who can thwart him? His hand is stretched out, and who can turn it back?[30]

Isa 43:13 "Yes, and from ancient days I am he. No one can deliver out of my hand. When I act, who can reverse it?"

Jer 32:17 "Sovereign Lord, you have made

[24]One of the most beautiful expressions of God's omnipresence in all Scripture. David realizes that his intensely personal relationship to God cannot be limited by space.

[25]Jeremiah warns the false prophets that no place can provide escape from the righteous judgment of God.

[26]Paul's speech at the Areopagus in Athens. God is in principle available to the "heathen" who have never heard the gospel; nature and conscience testify to his reality (Ro 1:19–20; 2:14–15). Man's separation from God is not geographic, but moral and spiritual: "Your iniquities have separated you from your God; your sins have hidden his face from you, so that he will not hear" (Isa 59:2).

[27]The exercise of God's power is always consistent with his holy nature; thus God cannot will to end his own life and existence, or to lie (Tit 1:2, "God, who does not lie"), or to break his promises (Heb 6:17–18).

[28]God's promise to Abraham exceeded the normal human possibilities for childbearing.

[29]A prayer by King Jehoshaphat at a time when the armies of Moab and Ammon were attacking Judah. In times of trouble and weakness men turn to God's power for help: "For we have no power to face this vast army that is attacking us. We do not know what to do, but our eyes are upon you" (20:12).

[30]The obvious answer to this rhetorical question is, "No one."

the heavens and the earth by your great power and outstretched arm. Nothing is too hard for you."[13]

Da 4:35 All the peoples of the earth are regarded as nothing. He does as he pleases with the powers of heaven and the peoples of the earth. No one can hold back his hand or say to him: "What have you done?"

Mk 10:27 Jesus looked at them and said, "With man this is impossible, but not with God; all things are possible with God."[32]

Eph 1:19–20 . . . his incomparably great power for us who believe. That power is like the working of his mighty strength, which he exerted in Christ when he raised him from the dead and seated him at his right hand in the heavenly realms. . . .[33]

Omniscience

God knows all things past, present and future, and all things possible as well as actual.

Ps 139:1–4 O Lord, you have searched me and you know me. You know when I sit and when I rise; you perceive my thoughts from afar. You discern my going out and my lying down; you are familiar with all my ways. Before a word is on my tongue you know it completely, O Lord.[34]

Isa 40:28 Do you not know? Have you not heard? The Lord is the everlasting God, the Creator of the ends of the earth. He will not grow tired or weary, and his understanding no one can fathom.

Isa 46:10 "I make known the end from the beginning, from ancient times, what is still to come. I say: My purpose will stand, and I will do all that I please."[35]

Rom 11:33 Oh, the depths of the riches of the wisdom and knowledge of God! How unsearchable his judgments, and his paths beyond tracing out!

Heb 4:13 Nothing in all creation is hidden

[31]A prayer of Jeremiah. At the time when the Babylonians were besieging Jerusalem, and Judah's position seemed hopeless, Jeremiah was instructed to purchase a field, as a symbol of Israel's eventual restoration.

[32]Jesus had just told the disciples that it was easier for a camel to go through the eye of a needle than for a rich man to enter the kingdom of God (10:25). Salvation is impossible for anyone on human strength or merit; every true conversion is the product of the supernatural power of God's Spirit (cf. Jn 1:13, "children born not of natural descent, nor of human decision or a husband's will, but born of God").

[33]The same divine power exercised in the creation of the universe has been manifested in the resurrection of Jesus Christ from the dead. The apostle Paul prays that the believing church might experience that same mighty power in its life and mission.

[34]God knows his children intimately. Even the very hairs of their head are numbered (Mt 10:30). This pervasive knowledge on God's part is intended to be a comfort and source of security to his people.

[35]God's omniscience and sovereign control of history are the foundation for predictive prophecy in Scripture. The inspired prophet can predict the future, because he speaks on behalf of the God who knows all things past, present, and future.

from God's sight. Everything is uncovered and laid bare before the eyes of him to whom we must give account.[36]

MORAL ATTRIBUTES

Those characteristics of the divine nature which are in some measure reflected in the creature.

1. *Holiness*

God's exaltation in majesty above the creation; his complete freedom from all moral impurity and imperfection.

Ex 15:11 "Who among the gods is like you, O Lord? Who is like you—majestic in holiness, awesome in glory, working wonders?"[37]

Lev 11:44 "I am the Lord your God; consecrate yourselves and be holy, because I am holy.' "[38]

Ps 22:3 Yet you are enthroned as the Holy One; you are the praise of Israel.[39]

Is 6:3 "Holy, holy, holy is the Lord Almighty; the whole earth is full of his glory."[40]

1Pe 1:15 Just as he who called you is holy, so be holy in all you do.[41]

Rev. 4:8 "Holy, holy, holy is the Lord God Almighty, who was, and is, and is to come."[42]

2. *Love*

God has strong affection for his children, and is positively committed to meeting their needs.

Dt 33:12 "Let the beloved of the Lord rest secure in him, for he shields him all day long, and the one the Lord loves rests between his shoulders."[43]

Ps 42:8 By day the Lord directs his love, at night his song is with me—a prayer to the God of my life.

[36]God's omniscience is a basis for his righteous judgment, both within history and at the last day. Unlike human judges, God has complete and perfect knowledge of man's heart and circumstances.

[37]From the song of Moses and the Israelites celebrating God's victory over Pharaoh and his army at the Red Sea. Frequently in Scripture God's holiness is manifested in his acts of power and judgment.

[38]God's holiness is to be reflected in the lives of his people.

[39]An alternative translation is "Yet you are holy, enthroned on the praises of Israel."

[40]Isaiah's temple vision. The threefold repetition emphasizes the centrality of holiness in this revelation of God's character.

[41]In the following verse Peter cites Lev 11:44–45. In the New Testament, the primary manifestations of God's holiness are to be found in Jesus Christ and the Holy Spirit.

[42]The unending praise offered by the living creatures in the throneroom of heaven.

[43]Just prior to his death Moses blesses the tribes of Israel. This quotation refers to the tribe of Benjamin.

Ps 63:3 Because your love is better than life, my lips will glorify you.[44]

Jer 31:3 "I have loved you with an everlasting love; I have drawn you with loving-kindness."[45]

**Jn 3:16* For God so loved the world that he gave his one and only Son,[46] that whoever believes in him shall not perish but have eternal life.

Ro 5:8 But God demonstrates his own love for us in this: While we were still sinners, Christ died for us.[47]

Eph 2:4–5 Because of his great love for us, God, who is rich in mercy, made us alive with Christ even when we were dead in transgressions—it is by grace you have been saved.

1Jn 4:10 This is love: not that we loved God, but that he loved us and sent his Son as an atoning sacrifice[48] for our sins.

3. *Wisdom*

"the virtue of God which manifests itself in the selection of worthy ends and in the choice of the best means for the realization of those ends" (Berkhof).

Ps 104:24 How many are your works, O Lord! In wisdom you made them all; the earth is full of your creatures.[49]

**Ps 147:5* Great is our Lord and mighty in power; his understanding has no limit.

Jer 10:7 Who should not revere you, O King of the nations? This is your due. Among all the wise men of the nations and in all their kingdoms, there is no one like you.

Da 2:20–21 "Praise be to the name of God forever and ever; wisdom and power are his. He changes times and seasons; he sets up kings and deposes them. He gives wisdom to the wise and knowledge to the discerning."[50]

Ro 11:33 Oh, the depth of the riches of the

[44]The traditional ascription to this psalm reads "A psalm of David. When he was in the desert of Judah." In a situation of personal extremity, David values the love of God more than any temporal benefits.

[45]The context speaks of the restoration of Israel after judgment and exile, and the new covenant that God will make with his people (vv. 33–34). As in Jn 3:16, the love of God is here a central motivation for God's saving purposes.

[46]Or, "his only begotten Son" *(ton huion ton monogenē).* Jesus is the unique Son of the Father.

[47]God takes the initiative in love, loving those who can claim no merit or favor in and of themselves. The *erōs* of the Greek tradition responds to attractive features in the beloved; the *agapē* of the God of the Bible is love for the unlovely.

[48]Or, "propitiation" *(hilasmon).* Propitiation is the averting of the wrath of an offended party by the offering of a gift. For a human example, recall the encounter of Jacob and Esau in Ge 32:17–21, where Jacob offers gifts to appease his brother's anger. In the NT, God is both the offended party and the provider of the gift.

[49]God's wisdom is displayed in the variety and complexity of the creation. This is a major theme in the Book of Job, and is the background of Ro 1:20: the unbeliever is without excuse in denying God's existence, power, and wisdom.

[50]The wisdom of God is manifested not only in the creation, but also in his

wisdom and knowledge of God! How unsearchable his judgments, and his paths beyond tracing out![51]

Col 2:2–3 My purpose [Paul's ministry] is that they may be encouraged in heart and united in love, so that they may have the full riches of complete understanding, in order that they may know the mystery of God, namely, Christ, in whom are hidden all the treasures of wisdom and knowledge.[52]

4. *Grace and Mercy*

Two closely related aspects of the divine nature. God's *grace* is his unmerited favour manifested in the forgiveness of sin; God's *mercy* is shown in the remission of punishment and in his disposition to relieve the misery caused by sin.

Ne 9:17 "But you are a forgiving God, gracious and compassionate, slow to anger and abounding in love."[53]

Ps 103:8 The Lord is compassionate and gracious, slow to anger, abounding in love.

Lk 1:54–55 "He has helped his servant Israel, remembering to be merciful to Abraham and his descendants forever, even as he said to our fathers."[54]

Ro 9:16 It [salvation] does not, therefore, depend on man's desire or effort, but on God's mercy.

Eph 1:6 To the praise of his glorious grace, which he has freely given us in the One he loves.

Eph 2:4–5 But because of his great love for us, God, who is rich in mercy, made us alive with Christ even when we were dead in transgressions—it is by grace you have been saved.[55]

Tit 2:11 For the grace of God that brings salvation has appeared to all men.[56]

Tit 3:5 He saved us, not because of righteous things we had done, but because of his mercy.

providential control of history.

[51]God's remarkable way of using the unbelief of Israel to bring the gospel to the Gentiles provoked this expression of praise by the apostle. God's ways of doing things often confound human plans and wisdom. "As the heavens are higher than the earth, so are my ways higher than your ways and my thoughts than your thoughts" (Isa 55:9).

[52]The wisdom of God, manifested in creation and history, is manifested preeminently in Jesus Christ, the supreme embodiment of the limitless wisdom of the Creator.

[53]In his prayer Nehemiah had previously mentioned Israel's stubbornness and rebellion.

[54]From Mary's song (the "Magnificat").

[55]Here, as frequently in Scripture, God's grace and mercy are closely associated.

[56]Not universal salvation (universalism), but the news of salvation is intended for all.

5. Goodness

The disposition of God to deal generously and benevolently with all his creatures.

Ps 100:5 For the Lord is good and his love endures forever; his faithfulness continues through all generations.

Ps 145:8–9 The Lord is gracious and compassionate, slow to anger and rich in love. The Lord is good to all; he has compassion on all he has made.

La 3:25 The Lord is good to those whose hope is in him, to the one who seeks him.

Mt 5:45 "He [God] causes his sun to rise on the evil and the good, and sends rain on the righteous and the unrighteous."[57]

Mt 7:11 "If you, then, though you are evil, know how to give good gifts to your children, how much more will your Father in heaven give good gifts to those who ask him!"[58]

Ac 14:17 "Yet he has not left himself without testimony: He has shown kindness by giving you rain from heaven and crops in their seasons; he provides you with plenty of food and fills your hearts with joy."[59]

Ja 1:5, 17 If any of you lacks wisdom, he should ask God, who gives generously to all without finding fault, and it will be given to him . . . Every good and perfect gift is from above, coming down from the Father of the heavenly lights, who does not change like shifting shadows.[60]

[57]God shows benevolence and generosity even to his enemies.

[58]Christ here points to the goodness of God as an *encouragement to prayer.*

[59]Paul and Barnabas in Lystra and Derbe. God's goodness is not limited to Israel or the church.

[60]God is the ultimate source of all goodness in human experience. This realization evokes praise from the believer: "Praise God from whom all blessings flow. . . ."

6. Patience

God's restraint of his righteous wrath and judgment in the face of rebellion and sin; divine forbearance.

Nu 14:18 "The Lord is slow to anger, abounding in love and forgiving sin and rebellion.' "

Ps 86:15 But you, O Lord, are a compassionate and gracious God, slow to anger, abounding in love and faithfulness.

Ro 2:4 Do you show contempt for the riches of his kindness, tolerance and patience, not realizing that God's kindness leads you towards repentance?[61]

[61]The term used here, *makrothumia,* can also have the connotation of "steadfastness" or "endurance" when describing a human character trait: Heb. 6:12; Jas. 5:10.

Ro 9:22 What if God, choosing to show his wrath and make his power known, bore with great patience the objects of his wrath—prepared for destruction?

2Pe 3:9 The Lord is not slow in keeping his promise, as some understand slowness. He is patient with you, not wanting anyone to perish, but everyone to come to repentance.

2Pe 3:14–15 So then, dear friends, since you are looking forward to this [day of the Lord, v.10], make every effort to be found spotless, blameless and at peace with him. Bear in mind that our Lord's patience means salvation, just as our dear brother Paul also wrote you with the wisdom that God gave him.

7. Righteousness and Justice

God's righteousness refers to the absolute moral rectitude of his commandments, promises, and actions; his justice is demonstrated in the complete equity and impartiality of his judicial acts.[62]

[62]Key biblical terms here include *tsedeq, tsᵉdaqah,* "righteousness": *dikaiosunē,* "righteousness" or "justice"; *mishpat,* "justice"; *yashar,* "just."

Dt 32:4 He is the Rock, his works are perfect, and all his ways are just. A faithful God who does no wrong, upright and just is he.[63]

[63]From the song of Moses.

Ps 36:6 Your righteousness is like the mighty mountains, your justice like the great deep.

Ps 72:2 He will judge your people in righteousness, your afflicted ones with justice.[64]

[64]Characteristics of the Messiah, the ideal king.

Ps 89:14 Righteousness and justice are the foundation of your throne.

Ps 98:9 He [God] will judge the world in righteousness and the peoples with equity.

Ps 119:172 May my tongue sing of your word, for all your commands are righteous.

Ac 17:31 "For he [God] has set a day when he will judge the world with justice by the man [Christ] he has appointed."[65]

Ro 3:25–26 God presented him [Christ] as a sacrifice of atonement,[66] through faith in his blood. He did this to demonstrate his justice, because in his forbearance he had left the sins committed beforehand unpunished—he did it to demonstrate his justice at the present time, so as to be just and the one who justifies the man who has faith in Jesus.[67]

2Pe 1:1 Simon Peter, a servant and apostle of Jesus Christ, To those who through the righteousness of our God and Saviour Jesus Christ have received a faith as precious as ours.

8. Truthfulness

The complete veracity and dependability of God's character, words, and actions.[68]

Nu 23:19 "God is not a man, that he should lie, nor a son of man, that he should change his mind. Does he speak and then not act? Does he promise and not fulfil?"[69]

Ps 33:4 For the word of the Lord is right and true; he is faithful in all he does.

Ps 119:151 Yet you are near, O Lord, and all your commands are true.

Ps 119:160 All your words are true; all your righteous laws are eternal.[70]

Jn 14:6 Jesus answered, "I am the way and the truth and the life. No one comes to the Father except through me."[71]

Jn 17:17 "Sanctify them by the truth; your word is truth."[72]

Rom 3:3–4 What if some [Jews] did not have faith? Will their lack of faith nullify God's faithfulness? Not at all! Let God be true, and every man a liar. As it is written:

[65]Paul's speech in Athens. In the NT, the judicial authority of God in the OT (e.g. Ps 98:9) is transferred to Jesus Christ—an indication of his divine status.

[66]Or, "propitiation," *hilastērion,* turning aside of wrath."

[67]The OT teaching about the righteousness and justice of God provides the indispensable foundation for understanding the NT teaching concerning the atoning death of Christ and the sinner's justification through faith in that work. God's justice required that sin be punished; yet in his mercy, he provided Christ as our substitute to die in our place.

[68]Hebrew *ᵉmet,* "truth, faithfulness"; Greek *alētheia,* "truth"; *alēthēo,* "true, honest, reliable"; *alēthinos,* "true, sincere, veracious." God's truthfulness involves both his *veracity* (correspondence of word and act to reality) and his *reliability* (his word can be depended upon). See A. C. Thiselton, "Truth," in Colin Brown, ed., *New International Dictionary of NT Theology* 3:874–902.

[69]An oracle of Balaam, spoken to Balak.

[70]The words of God reflect God's own truthfulness and eternity.

[71]Jesus Christ is the truth of God incarnate.

[72]God's word is the standard of truth and the instrument of the believer's sanctification.

"So that you may be proved right in your words and prevail in your judging."[73]

Tit 1:1–2 Paul, a servant of God and an apostle of Jesus Christ for the faith of God's elect and the knowledge of the truth that leads to godliness—a faith and knowledge resting on the hope of eternal life, which God, who does not lie, promised before the beginning of time.[74]

9. *Faithfulness*

The utter reliability, firmness and constancy of God's character, commands, and promises; his determined, steadfast loyalty toward his people and his covenant.[75]

Dt 7:9 Know therefore that the Lord your God is God; he is the faithful God, keeping his covenant of love to a thousand generations of those who love him and keep his commandments.

Dt 32:4 He is the Rock, his works are perfect, and all his ways are just. A faithful God who does no wrong, upright and just is he.[76]

Jos 23:14 "Now I [Joshua] am about to go the way of all the earth. You know with all your heart and soul that not one of all the good promises the Lord your God gave you has failed. Every promise has been fulfilled; not one has failed.

Ps 89:1–2, 8 I will sing of the Lord's great love forever; with my mouth I will make your faithfulness known through all generations. I will declare that your love stands firm forever, that you established your faithfulness in heaven itself. . . . O Lord God Almighty, who is like you? You are mighty, O Lord, and your faithfulness surrounds you.

**La 3:22–23* Because of the Lord's great love we are not consumed, for his compassions never fail. They are new every morning; great is your faithfulness.

1Co 10:13 No temptation has seized you

[73]Here God's truthfulness clearly involves his faithfulness to his covenant promises to the Jews. Paul resumes this theme in chapters 9–11. The quotation in v. 4 is from Ps 51:4.

[74]God's veracity and reliability is the ground of the believer's assurance of salvation.

[75]Hebrew *ᵉmet,* "truth, faithfulness"; *emunah,* "stability, faithfulness"; *pistis,* "faithfulness, steadfastness"; *pistos,* "faithful, steady."

[76]A rock is a fitting symbol of the firmness and stability of God's character.

except what is common to man. And God is faithful; he will not let you be tempted beyond what you can bear. But when you are tempted, he will also provide a way out so that you can stand up under it.

1Th 5:23–24 May God himself, the God of peace, sanctify you through and through. May your whole spirit, soul and body be kept blameless at the coming of our Lord Jesus Christ. The one who calls you is faithful and he will do it.[77]

[77]God's faithfulness is also demonstrated in the believer's sanctification.

2Ti 2:13 If we are faithless, he will remain faithful, for he cannot disown himself.

Heb 10:23 Let us hold unswervingly to the hope we profess, for he who promised is faithful.

1Jn 1:9 If we confess our sins, he is faithful and just and will forgive us our sins and purify us from all unrighteousness.

Trinity

"This article is so far above the power of the human mind to grasp, or the tongue to express, that God, as the Father of his children, will pardon us when we stammer and lisp as best we can, if only our faith be pure and right. By this term, however, we would say that we believe the divine majesty to be three distinct persons of one true essence" (Martin Luther, Epistle Sermon, Trinity Sunday).

The biblical doctrine of the Trinity, a keystone of orthodox Christianity, can be summarized in three statements: there is one God and only one God; this one God exists eternally in three persons, Father, Son, and Holy Spirit; these three persons are completely equal, each fully possessing the divine nature or essence.

Since the deity of Christ is treated in chapter 6, and the deity of the Father is uncontested, this section will treat the deity and personality of the Holy Spirit, and general texts where trinitarian language is used.

PERSONALITY OF THE SPIRIT

In the NT the Spirit teaches, speaks,

intercedes, wills, and can be grieved, and hence is clearly a person.

Lk 12:11–12 "When you are brought before synagogues, rulers and authorities, do not worry about how you will defend yourselves or what you will say, for the Holy Spirit will teach you at that time what you should say."[78]

[78]Words of encouragement from Christ to the disciples for times of persecution.

Ac 13:2 [commissioning of Paul and Barnabas by the church at Antioch]: While they were worshipping the Lord and fasting, the Holy Spirit said, "Set apart for me Barnabas and Saul for the work to which I have called them."[79]

[79]The Spirit *speaks* and *calls.*

Ro 8:26 In the same way, the Spirit helps us in our weakness. We do not know what we ought to pray, but the Spirit himself intercedes for us with groans that words cannot express.

1Co 12:7, 11 Now to each one the manifestation of the Spirit is given for the common good. . . . All these are the work of one and the same Spirit, and he gives them to each one, just as he determines.

Eph 4:30 Do not grieve the Holy Spirit of God, with whom you were sealed for the day of redemption.

DEITY OF THE SPIRIT

Ps 139:7 Where can I go from your Spirit? Where can I flee from your presence?[80]

[80]The Spirit possesses the divine attribute of omnipresence.

Ac 5:3–4 Then Peter said, "Ananias, how is it that Satan has so filled your heart that you have lied to the Holy Spirit and have kept for yourself some of the money you received for the land? . . . You have not lied to men but to God. . . ."[81]

[81]Lying to the Holy Spirit = lying to God.

1Co 2:10–11 The Spirit searches all things, even the deep things of God. . . . no one knows the thoughts of God except the Spirit of God.[82]

[82]The Spirit possesses a knowledge of the mind of God that far surpasses finite, human knowledge.

1Cor 3:16 Don't you know that you yourselves are God's temple and that God's Spirit lives in you?

1Co 6:19 Do you not know that your body is a temple of the Holy Spirit, who is in you, whom you have received from God?[83]

Heb 9:14 How much more, then, will the blood of Christ, who through the eternal Spirit offered himself unblemished to God, cleanse our consciences from acts that lead to death, so that we may serve the living God![84]

GENERAL TEXTS

Mt 28:19 "Therefore go and make disciples of all nations, baptizing them in the name of the Father and of the Son and of the Holy Spirit."[85]

2Co 13:14 May the grace of the Lord Jesus Christ, and the love of God, and the fellowship of the Holy Spirit be with you all.

1Pe 1:1–2 Peter, an apostle of Jesus Christ, To God's elect . . . chosen according to the foreknowledge of God the Father, through the sanctifying work of the Spirit, for obedience to Jesus Christ and sprinkling by his blood.[86]

Election

God's eternal, gracious choice of particular individuals to be saved through the merits and work of Jesus Christ.[87]

ARMINIAN VIEW

In the Arminian tradition, God's election is understood as being "conditional," i.e. predicated on foreseen faith in the believer. God elects those whom he foresees will respond in faith to the gospel. The elect are chosen "not by absolute decree, but by acceptance of the conditions of the call . . . election is by those means which make men righteous and holy" (Wiley).[88]

[83]Note the parallelism of "God's temple" in 3:16 and "temple of the Holy Spirit" in 6:19.

[84]The Spirit possesses the attribute of eternity.

[85]In this baptismal formula, as well as in a benediction such as 2Co 13:14, the Spirit is placed on a level of equality with the Father and the Son.

[86]All three Persons are involved in the work of salvation.

[87]In biblical usage, election can also refer to God's choice of certain individuals (e.g. Moses, Cyrus, Jesus Christ) for a particular task, or to his choice of Israel as a servant-nation. Here the concern is with election of individuals to *eternal life. Predestination,* a related term, refers to God's control and direction of the actions of all moral agents, e.g. Acts 4:27–28: "Indeed Herod and Pontius Pilate met together with the Gentiles and the people of Israel in this city to conspire against your holy servant Jesus, whom you anointed. They did what your power and will had decided beforehand (*proōrisen,* "predestined," RSV) should happen."

[88]For recent treatments from an Arminian perspective, see Wiley, H. Orton, *Christian Theology* (1952), vol. 2, chapt. 26; Forster, Roger T., and Marston, V. Paul, *God's Strategy in Human History* (1973); Pinnock, Clark, ed., *Grace Unlimited* (1975).

Jos 24:14–15 "Now fear the Lord and serve him with all faithfulness. Throw away the gods your forefathers worshipped beyond the River and in Egypt, and serve the Lord. But if serving the Lord seems undesirable to you, then choose for yourselves this day whom you will serve, whether the gods your forefathers served beyond the River, or the gods of the Amorites, in whose land you are living. But as for me and my household, we will serve the Lord."[89]

Eze 33:11 " 'As surely as I live, declares the Sovereign Lord, I take no pleasure in the death of the wicked, but rather that they turn from their ways and live. Turn! Turn from your evil ways! Why will you die, O house of Israel?' "[90]

Mk 1:15 "The time has come," he [Jesus] said. "The kingdom of God is near. Repent and believe the good news!"[91]

Lk 7:28–30 "I tell you, among those born of women there is no greater than John [the Baptist]; yet the one who is least in the kingdom of God is greater than he." (All the people, even the tax collectors, when they heard Jesus' words, acknowledged that God's way was right, because they had been baptized by John. But the Pharisees and experts in the law rejected God's purpose for themselves, because they had not been baptized by John.)[92]

Jn 3:16 For God so loved the world that he gave his one and only Son, that whoever believes in him shall not perish but have eternal life.[93]

Ac 7:51 "You stiff-necked people, with uncircumcised hearts and ears! You are just like your fathers: You always resist the Holy Spirit!"[94]

Ro 8:29 For those God foreknew he also predestined to be conformed to the likeness of his Son, that he might be the firstborn among many brothers.[95]

Eph 1:4 For he [God] chose us in him [Christ] before the creation of the world to

[89]The covenant renewed under Joshua at Shechem. Man must make a conscious choice to serve God.

[90]Cited by John Wesley in the pamphlet, "Serious considerations on Absolute Predestination," with reference to the concept of an unconditional reprobation.

[91]The command to *repent* and *believe* implies the human ability to respond to the gospel, as assisted by the grace that God himself supplies (prevenient grace).

[92]The Pharisees *rejected God's purpose for themselves:* the context involves faith, repentance, and salvation.

[93]God's love extends to the entire world; only *unbelief* excludes the sinner from enjoying the saving benefits of the gospel.

[94]Stephen's speech to the Sanhedrin. The Spirit's converting influence can be resisted by the sinful human will.

[95]According to the Arminian view, God elects those whom he foresees will respond in faith to the gospel.

be holy and blameless in his sight.[96]

1Ti 2:3–4 This [prayer for all, v.1] is good, and pleases God our Savior, who wants all men to be saved and to come to a knowledge of the truth.[97]

1Pe 1:1–2 Peter, an apostle of Jesus Christ, To God's elect . . . who have been chosen according to the foreknowledge of God the Father, through the sanctifying work of the Spirit, for obedience to Jesus Christ and sprinkling by his blood.[98]

CALVINISTIC VIEW

In the Calvinistic tradition, God's election is understood as being "unconditional," i.e. not predicated on foreseen faith in the believer. God's antecedent election creates faith in the elect. "Those of mankind that are predestinated unto life, God, before the foundation of the world was laid . . . hath chosen in Christ, unto everlasting glory, out of his mere free grace and love, without any foresight of faith or good works . . ." (*West. Conf.* III.v).

2Ch 20:6 "Oh Lord, God of our fathers, are you not the God who is in heaven? You rule over all the kingdoms of the nations. Power and might are in your hand, and no one can withstand you."[99]

Isa 14:26–27 This is the plan determined for the whole world; this is the hand stretched out over all nations. For the Lord Almighty has purposed, and who can thwart him? His hand is stretched out, and who can turn it back?[100]

Isa 43:12–13 "You are my witnesses," declares the Lord, "that I am God. Yes, and from ancient days I am he. No one can deliver out of my hand. When I act, who can reverse it?"

Jn 6:37 "All that the Father gives me will come to me, and whoever comes to me I will never drive away."[101]

[96]See note 9 above on Ro 8:29.

[97]See note 6 above on Jn 3:16.

[98]God's election is manifested in a life of holiness and obedience.

[99]A prayer of King Jehoshaphat of Judah when the nation was being attacked by the Moabites and Ammonites, Men may resist for a season, but God's purpose prevails.

[100]A prophecy against the nation of Assyria and the pretensions of its leaders.

[101]From Christ's "Bread of Life" discourse. The Father's *giving* is prior to the believer's *coming.*

Jn 15:16 "You did not choose me, but I chose you to go and bear fruit—fruit that will last."[102]

Ac 13:46, 48 Then Paul and Barnabas answered them [the Jews] boldly: "We had to speak the word of God to you first. Since you reject it and do not consider yourselves worthy of eternal life, we now turn to the Gentiles. . . ." When the Gentiles heard this, they were glad and honoured the word of the Lord; and all who were appointed for eternal life believed.[103]

Ro 8:29 For those God foreknew he also predestined to be conformed to the likeness of his Son, that he might be the firstborn among many brothers.[104]

Ro 9:10–12, 16 Not only that, but Rebecca's children had one and the same father, our father Isaac. Yet before the twins were born or had done anything good or bad—in order that God's purpose in election might stand: not by works but by him who calls—she was told, "The older will serve the younger. . . ." It [God's election] does not, therefore, depend on man's desire or effort, but on God's mercy.[105]

Eph 1:4 For he chose us in him before the creation of the world to be holy and blameless in his sight.[106]

[102]From Christ's discourse to the disciples on the "Vine and the Branches." The disciple's response to Christ is a consequence of the Lord's prior call.

[103]Paul and Barnabas in the synagogue in Pisidian Antioch. God's appointment to eternal life is the foundation of the faith-response.

[104]In the Calvinistic view, God's foreknowing and electing are virtually synonymous; God does not elect on the basis of foreseen faith—rather, his election produces faith.

[105]The "bottom line" of election is God's mercy, not human desire or effort. From an Arminian perspective, Jacob and Esau are representatives of the *nations* of Israel and Edom; the text refers to national election rather than to the eternal election of individuals.

[106]See note 18 on Ro 8:29.

FOR FURTHER READING

General

Bavinck, H. *The doctrine of God* (1951), 407pp. (C)

Kaiser, C. M. *The doctrine of God: an historical survey* (Foundations for Faith) (1982), 152pp. (C)

Wood, A. S. *What the Bible says about God* (1980), 111pp. (A)

Existence

HODGE, C. *Systematic Theology*, I, pp.191–237. (1872, many rep.) (C)
LITTON, E. A. *Introduction to dogmatic Theology*, sect. 8–24 (1902). (B)
WARD, K. *Holding fast to God* (1982), pp.1–49. ( )
KÜNG, H. *Does God exist?* (1980), 839pp. (C)

Attributes

CHARNOCK, S. *The attributes of God* (1682, many rep.), 800pp. (C)
PACKER, J. I. *Knowing God* (1973), 316pp. (B)
PHILLIPS, J. B. *Your God is too small* (1961), 127pp. (A)
TOZER, A. W. *The knowledge of the holy* (1961), 196pp. (A)

Trinity

FRANKS, R. S. *The doctrine of the Trinity* (1983), 201pp. (B)
OLYOTT, S. *The Three are one* (1980), 104pp. (A)
WARFIELD, B. B. "The Biblical doctrine of the Trinity", art. in *International Standard Bible Encyclopedia* (1915), pp.3012–3022. (B)

Election

art. "Predestination" by B. B. Warfield in *Hastings' Dictionary of the Bible*, IV, pp.47–63. (B)
God's strategy in human history, by R. T. Forster and V. P. Marston (1973), 236pp. (B)
PINNOCK, C. *ed. Grace unlimited* (1975), 264pp. (B)
BOETTNER, L. *The Reformed doctrine of predestination* (1932), 432pp. (C)

3

CREATION

"We believe in one God, the Father All Governing, creator of all things visible and invisible." These opening lines of the Nicene Creed (325) point to the foundational nature of the biblical doctrine of creation. The knowledge of God the Father, maker of heaven and earth, of *all things* visible and invisible, is the basis for understanding and appreciating the knowledge of God the Son, in Jesus Christ, as Lord and Saviour.

Ge 1:1 In the beginning God created the heavens and the earth.

Ne 9:5–6 "Blessed be your glorious name, and may it be exalted above all blessing and praise. You alone are the Lord. You made the heavens, even the highest heavens, and all their starry host, the earth and all that is on it, the seas and all that is in them. You give life to everything, and the multitudes of heaven worship you."[1]

Ps 33:6 By the word of the Lord were the heavens made, their starry host by the breath of his mouth.

Ps 90:2 Before the mountains were born or you brought forth the earth and the world, from everlasting to everlasting you are God.[2]

Pr 3:19 By wisdom the Lord laid the earth's foundations, by understanding he set the heavens in place.[3]

Isa 44:24 "This is what the Lord says—your Redeemer, who formed you in the womb: I am the Lord, who has made all things, who

[1]After Ezra's reading of the Law, the Levites lead the people in prayer. Here, as in other great prayers of the Bible, the prayer begins not with petitions addressed to God, but with an acknowledgment of God's power and character as revealed in creation.

[2]God is eternal: the universe is not. The biblical view of creation rules out both the eternal coexistence of God and matter and the confusion of God's essence with the world (pantheism). God created "ex nihilo," "out of nothing" (or, *into* nothing).

[3]God's attribute of *wisdom (hokhmah)* is displayed in the things which he has made. Cf. Ro 1:20: "For since the creation of the world God's invisible qualities—his eternal power and divine nature—have been clearly seen, being understood from what has been made."

alone stretched out the heavens, who spread out the earth by myself."[4]

[4]God's power to *redeem* presupposes his power to *create.*

Jer 32:17 "Sovereign Lord, you have made the heavens and the earth by your great power and outstretched arm. Nothing is too hard for you."[5]

[5]Even though the restoration of Israel from exile seems virtually impossible, humanly speaking, Jeremiah is reminded of God's infinite power as shown in his creation of the universe. God is greater than our circumstances and problems.

Jn 1:3 Through him [Christ] all things were made; without him nothing was made that has been made.[6]

[6]Jesus Christ was active in the creation of the world as well as in the salvation of his people.

Col 1:16 For by him [Christ] all things were created: things in heaven and on earth, visible and invisible, whether thrones or powers or rulers or authorities; all things were created by him and for him.[7]

[7]Spirit beings—angels, principalities, powers, and Satan himself—were created by God, and remain under his sovereign control.

Heb 1:2 But in these last days he has spoken to us by his Son, whom he appointed heir of all things, and through whom he made the universe.

Heb 11:3 By faith we understand that the universe was formed at God's command, so that what is seen was not made out of what was visible.[8]

[8]God created by the word of his power, *ex nihilo,* and not out of preexisting matter.

Rev 4:11 "You are worthy, our Lord and God, to receive glory and honour and power, for you created all things, and by your will they were created and have their being."[9]

[9]Proper recognition of God as Creator of the universe evokes worship and praise from God's creatures.

FOR FURTHER READING

Creation

BUSWELL, J. O. *A systematic Theology* (1962), pp.130–162. (A)
BARTH, K. *Dogmatics in outline,* ch. 8, "God the Creator" (1949), pp.50–58. (B)
BARTH, K. *Church Dogmatics: the doctrine of creation* (1958–61) 4 vols.! (C)
HOLMES, A. *Contours of a world view* (1983), ch. 4 & 5. (B)
HOUSTON, J. M. *I believe in the Creator* (1979), 288pp. (B)

Creation and evolution

Creation and evolution, ed. D. C. Burke (1984), 288pp. ('When Christians disagree' series) (B)

4

PROVIDENCE

"When [faith] . . . has learned that he is the Creator of all things, it should immediately conclude that he is also their perpetual governor and preserver. . . . All the parts of the world are quickened by the secret inspiration of God" (John Calvin, *Institutes,* I.xvi.1).

Providence is that sovereign activity of God whereby he sustains, preserves, and governs all his creatures, and guides all events toward their appointed ends. God's providential activity can be seen in nature, in world history, and in personal circumstances. By the providence of God all events of nature and history are directed toward the fulfilment of his eternal plan of salvation.

Nature[1]

Job 5:10 "He bestows rain on the earth; he sends water upon the countryside."

Ps 65:9–10 You care for the land and water it; you enrich it abundantly. The streams of God are filled with water to provide the people with grain, for so you have ordained it. You drench its furrows and level its ridges; you soften it with showers and bless its crops.

Ps 104:14 He makes grass grow for the cattle, and plants for man to cultivate.

Ps 147:8–9 He covers the sky with clouds; he supplies the earth with rain and makes grass grow on the hills. He provides food for

[1]The moral and spiritual purposes of God are expressed through the secondary causes (laws of nature) over which he is sovereign.

the cattle and for the young ravens when they call.

Jer 10:13 When he thunders, the waters in the heavens roar; he makes clouds rise from the ends of the earth. He sends lightning with the rain and brings out the wind from his storehouses.

Hag 2:17 "I struck all the work of your hands with blight, mildew, and hail, yet you did not turn to me,' declares the Lord."[2]

Mt 6:26 "Look at the birds of the air; they do not sow or reap or store away in barns, and yet your heavenly Father feeds them. Are you not much more valuable than they?"[3]

Ac 14:17 "Yet he has not left himself without testimony: He has shown kindness by giving you rain from heaven and crops in their seasons; he provides you with plenty of food and fills your hearts with joy."[4]

[2]God, through his control of the weather and the elements of nature, sends judgment upon agriculture to recall his people to covenant obedience.

[3]God's providential care for the birds is a source of assurance for anxious disciples.

[4]Paul and Barnabas at Lystra, on the first missionary tour.

World History

Job 12:23–24 "He makes nations great, and destroys them; he enlarges nations, and disperses them. He deprives the leaders of the earth of their reason; he sends them wandering through a trackless waste."

Ps 22:28 Dominion belongs to the Lord and he rules over the nations.

Jer 27:5–6 "With my great power and outstretched arm I made the earth and its people and the animals that are on it, and I give it to anyone I please. Now I will hand all your countries over to my servant Nebuchadnezzar king of Babylon; I will make even the wild animals subject to him."

Da 2:21 "He changes times and seasons; he sets up kings and deposes them. He gives wisdom to the wise and knowledge to the discerning."

Da 4:17 " '. . . the Most High is sovereign over the kingdoms of men and gives them to anyone he wishes and sets over them the lowliest of men.' "

Ac 4:27–28 "Indeed Herod and Pontius Pilate met together with the Gentiles and the people of Israel in this city to conspire against your holy servant Jesus, whom you anointed. They did what your power and will had decided beforehand should happen."[5]

Ac 17:25–27 "And he is not served by human hands, as if he needed anything, because he himself gives all men life and breath and everything else. From one man he made every nation of men . . . he determined the times set for them and the exact places where they should live."[6]

Personal circumstances

Ge 45:8; 50:20 "So then, it was not you who sent me [Joseph] here, but God. He made me father to Pharaoh, lord of his entire household and ruler of all Egypt . . . You intended to harm me, but God intended it for good to accomplish what is now being done, the saving of many lives."[7]

Job 14:5 "Man's days are determined; you have decreed the number of his months and have set limits he cannot exceed."

Ps 139:16 All the days ordained for me were written in your book before one of them came to be.[8]

Mt 10:29–31 "Are not two sparrows sold for a penny? Yet not one of them will fall to the ground apart from the will of your Father. And even the very hairs of your head are all numbered. So don't be afraid; you are worth more than many sparrows."

**Ro 8:28* And we know that in all things God works for the good of those who love him, who have been called according to his purpose.

[5]The crucifixion of Jesus by lawless men, by the providence of God, serves and fulfils the plan of salvation.

[6]In his evangelistic sermon in Athens, Paul points to God's revelation in creation and providence.

[7]God turned the evil intentions of Joseph's brothers toward the service of his own redemptive purposes.

[8]In vv. 13–16 David realizes that God's "plan for his life" began in his mother's womb.

FOR FURTHER READING

Providence

art. "Providence" by J. I. Packer, in *New Bible Dictionary* (1962), pp.1050–52. (B)
art. "Providence" by W. F. Tillett, in *ISBE* (1915), pp.2476–2485. (B)
STRONG, A. H. *Systematic Theology* (1907), pp.419–443. (B)
FLAVEL, J. *The mystery of providence* (1678, many rep.) (A)

Evil

Encountering evil: live options in theodicy, ed. S. T. Davis (1981). (B)
WENHAM, J. W. *The goodness of God* (1974), 223pp. (B)

5

MAN

" 'God created man in his own image; in the image of God created he him.' . . . God did not make him mere matter, a piece of senseless, unintelligent clay; but a spirit, like himself, although clothed with a material vehicle" (John Wesley, *Sermons on the Fall of Man,* II,6).

The biblical doctrine of man includes the creation of men and women as image-bearers of God and as morally responsible creatures, the various constituent aspects of man's created nature, and human nature as disordered under the impact of sin.

Man's Original State

God created man and woman in his own image and likeness. Creation in the image and likeness of God included the moral and spiritual nature, intellect, feelings, will, and dominion over the lower creation. God created man and woman as morally responsible agents.

Ge 1:26–27 Then God said, "Let us make man in our image, in our likeness, and let them rule over the fish of the sea and the birds of the air, over the livestock, over all the earth, and over all the creatures that move along the ground." So God created man in his own image, in the image of God he created him; male and female he created them.[1]

Ge 2:18, 15 Now the Lord God had planted a garden in the east, in Eden; and there he put the man he had formed. . . . The Lord God

[1]The Scriptures never give an explicit definition of the image *tselem)* and likeness *(d^emut),* but the features mentioned above are implicit in the biblical texts. As God's image-bearers men and women have cultural tasks, the calling to be God's vice-regents, stewards, and rulers on earth.

took the man and put him in the Garden of Eden to work it and take care of it.[2]

Ge 9:6 "Whoever sheds the blood of man, by man shall his blood be shed; for in the image of God has God made man."[3]

Ps 8:3–6 When I consider your heavens, the work of your fingers, the moon and the stars, which you have set in place, what is man that you are mindful of him, the son of man that you care for him? You made him a little lower than the heavenly beings and crowned him with glory and honour. You made him ruler over the works of your hands; you put everything under his feet. . . .[4]

Ecc 7:29 "This only have I found: God made mankind upright, but men have gone in search of many schemes."[5]

Ac 17:26 "From one man he made every nation of men, that they should inhabit the whole earth; and he determined the times set for them and the exact places where they should live."[6]

Ro 2:14–15 Indeed, when Gentiles, who do not have the law, do by nature things required by the law, they are a law for themselves, even though they do not have the law, since they show that the requirements of the law are written on their hearts, their consciences also bearing witness, and their thoughts now accusing, now even defending them.[7]

Jas 3:9–10 With the tongue we praise our Lord and Father, and with it we curse men, who have been made in God's likeness. Out of the same mouth come praise and cursing. My brothers, this should not be.[8]

[2]Man was not created for a life of idleness, but for a life of labour on God's behalf.

[3]The image of God is made the basis for the institution of capital punishment. An attack on man's bodily integrity is an attack on the majesty of God, man's creator. The text represents the Noahic rather than the Mosaic stage of revelation, and hence is not limited in its significance to Israel as a theocratic state.

[4]A poetic reflection on Ge 1:26–27: God's creation is immense, but man, as the crown of creation, has a dignity and grandeur that surpasses that of the cosmos.

[5]Mankind's moral devolution should not be blamed on God.

[6]All races of mankind share a common human nature, being descendants of Adam.

[7]All people, even those without access to biblical revelation, are morally responsible agents, being endowed with a God-created conscience that reflects the requirements of the moral law.

[8]Disrespect for any man or woman is inconsistent with that person's status as an image-bearer of God.

Aspects of Human Nature

Biblical scholars debate whether the Bible teaches that human nature is composed of three basic aspects (body, soul, spirit: "trichotomy") or of two (body and soul, or body and spirit:

"dichotomy"). In any case, the Bible emphasizes the unity of man's total life in the presence of God.

TRICHOTOMY

1Co 14:14 If I pray in a tongue, my spirit prays, but my mind is unfruitful.[9]

1Th 5:23 May God himself, the God of peace, sanctify you through and through. May your whole spirit, soul and body be kept blameless at the coming of our Lord Jesus Christ.

Heb 4:12 The word of God is living and active. Sharper than any double-edged sword, it penetrates even to dividing soul and spirit, joints and marrow; it judges the thoughts and attitudes of the heart.[10]

DICHOTOMY

Ge 2:7 And the Lord God formed man from the dust of the ground and breathed into his nostrils the breath of life, and man became a living being.[11]

Mt 10:28 "Do not be afraid of those who kill the body but cannot kill the soul. Rather, be afraid of the one who can destroy both soul and body in hell."[12]

Lk 1:46–47 And Mary said: "My soul praises the Lord and my spirit rejoices in God my Saviour."[13]

2Co 7:1 Since we have these promises, dear friends, let us purify ourselves from everything that contaminates body and spirit, perfecting holiness out of reverence for God.[14]

[9]The apostle appears to distinguish the spirit *(pneuma)* and the mind *(nous)* in this text.

[10]The writer distinguishes soul and spirit, as he does joints and marrow.

[11]Two basic aspects are mentioned: the material, dust *(aphar),* and the immaterial, the breath of life *(nishmat hayim).* Man as a whole is constituted a living being, lit. a "living soul" *(nefesh hayyah).*

[12]The totality of human existence is referred to in terms of body and soul.

[13]Mary's song, the "Magnificat." Verses 46 and 47 are an example of Hebrew parallelism; soul and spirit are functionally equivalent.

[14]In this text the apostle speaks of complete sanctification in terms of body and spirit.

Man in the State of Sin

ORIGINAL SIN

The sinfulness, guilt, and susceptibility to death inherited by all human beings (Christ excepted) from Adam.

"Our old man—Coeval with our being, and as old as the fall, our evil nature; a strong and beautiful expression for that entire

depravity and corruption, which by nature spreads itself over the whole man, leaving no part uninfected" (John Wesley, Notes on Rom 6:6).

Ge 2:16–17 And the Lord God commanded the man, "You are free to eat from any tree in the garden; but you must not eat from the tree of the knowledge of good and evil, for when you eat of it you will surely die."[15]

Job 14:1,4 "Man born of woman is of few days and full of trouble. . . . Who can bring what is pure from the impure? No one!"

Ps 51:5 Surely I have been a sinner from birth, sinful from the time my mother conceived me.[16]

Ps 58:3 Even from birth the wicked go astray; from the womb they are wayward and speak lies.

Ro 5:12,18–19 Therefore, just as sin entered the world through one man, and death through sin, and in this way death came to all men, because all sinned. . . . just as the result of one trespass was condemnation for all men, so also the result of one act of righteousness was justification that brings life for all men. For just as through the disobedience of the one man the many were made sinners, so also through the obedience of the one man the many will be made righteous.[17]

1Co 15:22 For as in Adam all die, so in Christ all will be made alive.[18]

Eph 2:3 All of us also lived among them at one time, gratifying the cravings of our sinful nature and following its desires and thoughts. Like the rest, we were by nature objects of wrath.[19]

PERSONAL SIN

The various sins committed by individuals subsequent to Adam's original sin. The Scriptures clearly teach that all persons actually commit such sins.[20]

1Ki 8:46 "When they sin against you—for

[15]The "covenant of works" made with Adam, who represented the human race as its federal head (cf. Ro 5:12–21).

[16]David's confession of sin after his adultery with Bathsheba. The sinful state long preceded the sinful act. Note that the text does not state that human sexuality is *per se* sinful; sexuality, however, like all other aspects of human nature, has been infected by sin.

[17]The comparison of the disobedience of Adam and the obedience of Christ. See vv. 12–21 for the complete comparison. Throughout, the emphasis is on the impact of the disobedience of the *one man* (Adam) that brought condemnation and death upon the human race. The Pelagian interpretation of v.12, taking "because all sinned" as subsequent *individual* sins, rather than "all sinned (in Adam)," destroys the force of the comparison, which stresses the impact of the sin of the *one man* (cf. vv. 12, 15, 16, 17, 19).

[18]The passage does not teach universal salvation. Those who are *in Adam* (the entire fallen race) are under the sentence of death; only those who are *in Christ* will be made alive. Note v.17, faith in Christ; v.18, those who have died *in Christ* (i.e., as believers).

[19]The phrase "by nature" *(phusei)* also appears in Ro. 2:14, where the Gentiles are said to occasionally do by nature the things of the law. See also 1 Co 11:14. The reference to *phusis* implies a congenital capacity,

there is no one who does not sin. . . ."[21]

Pr 20:9 Who can say, "I have kept my heart pure; I am clean and without sin"?[22]

**Ro 3:23* For all have sinned and fall short of the glory of God. . . .

1Jn 1:8 If we claim to be without sin, we deceive ourselves and the truth is not in us.

rather than an acquired one.

[20]Sometimes also called "actual" sin. This terminology, however, suggests that original sin is in some sense less real—which is definitely not the case.

[21]From Solomon's prayer of dedication for the temple.

[22]The answer, clearly, is "no one."

MANIFESTATIONS AND CONSEQUENCES OF SIN

The Scriptures teach that sin produces physical and spiritual death, alienation from God, spiritual blindness and hardness of heart, violence, licentiousness, social injustice, together with many other acts and attitudes destructive of human life and relationships.

Ge 6:5 The Lord saw how great man's wickedness on the earth had become, and that every inclination of the thoughts of his heart was only evil all the time.[23]

Pr 22:15 Folly is bound up in the heart of a child, but the rod of discipline will drive it far from him.[24]

Am 5:12 For I know how many are your offences and how great your sins. You oppress the righteous and take bribes and you deprive the poor of justice in the courts.[25]

Mt 15:19 "For out of the heart come evil thoughts, murder, adultery, sexual immorality, theft, false testimony, slander."[26]

Ro 6:23 For the wages of sin is death, but the gift of God is eternal life in Christ Jesus our Lord.

Ro 7:14–15 We know that the law is spiritual; but I am unspiritual, sold as a slave to sin. I do not understand what I do. For what I want to do I do not do, but what I hate I do.[27]

Ro 8:7–8 The sinful mind is hostile to God. It does not submit to God's law, nor can it do

[23]The prelude to God's universal judgment by the Flood.

[24]Even a young child's acts demonstrate that he does not enter the world with a neutral human nature; positive discipline is required to curb the sinful bent.

[25]Sin manifests itself in social as well as private acts.

[26]Man's *heart,* not his physical or socioeconomic environment, is the root source of sinful and antisocial behaviour.

[27]Sin produces not merely specific sinful acts, but a state of spiritual bondage.

so. Those controlled by the sinful nature cannot please God.[28]

[28]The sinful nature produces hostility to God and his law. Spiritual neutrality toward God is not a possibility.

Gal 5:19–21 The acts of the sinful nature are obvious: sexual immorality, impurity and debauchery; idolatry and witchcraft; hatred, discord, jealousy, fits of rage, selfish ambition, dissensions, factions and envy; drunkenness, orgies, and the like. I warn you, as I did before, that those who live like this will not inherit the kingdom of God.

Eph 4:17–19 . . . you must no longer live as the Gentiles do, in the futility of their thinking. They are darkened in their understanding and separated from the life of God because of the ignorance that is in them due to the hardening of their hearts. Having lost all sensitivity, they have given themselves over to sensuality so as to indulge in every kind of impurity, with a continual lust for more.[29]

[29]A life of sin leads to spiritual blindness and insensitivity ("noetic effects of sin"), which in turn leads to further sin and sensuality.

1Ti 4:1–2 The Spirit clearly says that in later times some will abandon the faith and follow deceiving spirits and things taught by demons. Such teachings come through hypocritical liars, whose consciences have been seared as with a hot iron.[30]

[30]Continual sin and violation of the conscience leads to a deadening of the conscience.

Rev 21:8 "But the cowardly, the unbelieving, the vile, the murderers, the sexually immoral, those who practice magic arts, the idolaters and all liars—their place will be in the fiery lake of burning sulphur. This is the second death."[31]

[31]The ultimate outcome of a life of unrepentant sin. The first death is physical, the second spiritual.

FOR FURTHER READING

Man

Carey, G. *I believe in man* (1977), 190pp. (A)
Cave, S. *The Christian estimate of man* (1944) (Mainly historical) 235pp. (B)
Berkouwer, G. C. *Man: the image of God* (1962), 376pp. (C)
Laidlaw, J. *The Bible doctrine of man* (1905), 364pp. (B)
Niebuhr, R. *The nature and destiny of man* (1941), 2 vols. (C)

Sin

BERKOUWER, G. C. *Sin* (1971), 600pp. (C)
LUTHER, M. *The bondage of the will* (tr. and ed. by J. I. Packer and O. R. Johnston) (1957), 323pp. (B)
Orr, J. *Sin as a problem today* (1910), 324pp. (B)
art, "Sin" in *New International Dictionary of New Testament Theology* (1978), III, 573–587. (B)
MACKINTOSH, R. *Christianity and sin* (1913), 231pp. (B)
DUBARLE, A. M. *Biblical doctrine of original sin* (1964), 245pp. (B)

6

PERSON OF CHRIST

"The history of the Church Universal has confirmed in me the conviction that those who have had and maintained the central article in its integrity, that of Jesus Christ, have remained safely entrenched in their Christian faith. . . . He who steadfastly holds to the doctrine that Jesus Christ is true God and true man, who died and rose again for us, will acquiesce in and heartily assent to all the other articles of the Christian faith" (Martin Luther, "Earliest Christian Creeds").

The person and work of Jesus Christ constitute the vital centre of Christian theology. This section will treat key texts relating to the preexistence, Virgin Birth, sinlessness, humanity and deity of the Saviour.

Preexistence

Jesus Christ, the unique Son of God, and second person of the Trinity, was not in his divine nature a creature of time, but was coequal with the Father from all eternity.

Isa 9:6 For to us a child is born, to us a son is given, and the government will be on his shoulders. And he will be called Wonderful Counsellor, Mighty God, Everlasting Father, Prince of Peace.[1]

Mic 5:2 "But you, Bethlehem Ephrathah, though you are small among the clans of Judah, out of you will come for me one who will be ruler over Israel, whose origins are from old, from ancient times."[2]

Jn 1:1–3 In the beginning was the Word,

[1]The Messiah, like God the Father, has an everlasting or eternal nature. The term "mighty God" (*El gibbor*) is used in 10:21 of the God of Israel, a strong indication of the divine nature of the Messiah whose birth is foretold in 9:6.

[2]The Messiah is to be born in Bethlehem. An alternate translation is "whose goings out are

and the Word was with God, and the Word was God. He was with God in the beginning. Through him all things were made; without him nothing was made that has been made.[3]

Jn 6:38 "For I have come down from heaven not to do my will but to do the will of him who sent me."[4]

Jn 8:56–58 "Your Father Abraham rejoiced at the thought of seeing my day; he saw it and was glad." "You are not yet fifty years old," the Jews said to him, "and you have seen Abraham!" "I tell you the truth," Jesus answered, "before Abraham was born, I am!"[5]

Jn 17:4–5 "I have brought you glory on earth by completing the work you gave me to do. And now, Father, glorify me in your presence with the glory I had with you before the world began."[6]

Gal 4:4–5 But when the time had fully come, God sent his Son, born of a woman, born under law, to redeem those under law, that we might receive the full rights of sons.

Php 2:5–7 Your attitude should be the same as that of Christ Jesus: Who, being in very nature God, did not consider equality with God something to be grasped, but made himself nothing, taking the very nature of a servant, being made in human likeness.[7]

Rev 22:12,13,16 "Behold, I am coming soon. . . . I am the Alpha and the Omega, the First and the Last, the Beginning and the End. . . . I, Jesus, have sent my angel to give you this testimony for the churches."[8]

from old, from days of eternity."

[3]The Word stands on the side of the Creator, not the creation; He was not a part of creation, but the co-author of creation. Cf. Col 1:15–16.

[4]From the bread of life discourse.

[5]The unbelieving Jews recognized the use of the "I am" language as an implicit claim to deity, and were prepared to stone Jesus for what they considered blasphemy (v. 59).

[6]From the "High Priestly Prayer" of Jesus prior to his betrayal and arrest.

[7]The "self-emptying" (v. 7, *ekenōsen*) of Christ involved not a lessening of his divine nature, but his voluntary assumption of the form of a servant in the incarnation.

[8]In 1:8 the term "Alpha and Omega" is used of the Lord God; in 22:13 of Christ.

Virgin Birth

Jesus Christ was conceived by the Holy Spirit, supernaturally apart from a human father, and born of the Virgin Mary. From the very beginning, the incarnation of Christ, like salvation itself, was the sovereign, supernatural initiative of God, beyond all merely human possibilities.

Isa 7:14 "Therefore the Lord himself will

give you a sign: The virgin[9] will be with child and will give birth to a son, and will call him Immanuel."

Mt 1:18–25 This is how the birth of Jesus Christ came about. His mother Mary was pledged to be married to Joseph, but before they came together, she was found to be with child through the Holy Spirit. Because Joseph her husband was a righteous man and did not want to expose her to public disgrace, he had in mind to divorce her quietly. But after he had considered this, an angel of the Lord appeared to him in a dream and said, "Joseph son of David, do not be afraid to take Mary home as your wife, because what is conceived in her is from the Holy Spirit. She will give birth to a son, and you are to give him the name Jesus, because he will save his people from their sins." All this took place to fulfil what the Lord had said through the prophet: "The virgin will be with child and will give birth to a son, and they will call him Immanuel"—which means, "God with us." When Joseph woke up, he did what the angel of the Lord had commanded him and took Mary home as his wife. But he had no union with her until she gave birth to a son. And he gave him the name Jesus.

Lk 1:26–38 In the sixth month, God sent the angel Gabriel to Nazareth, a town in Galilee, to a virgin[10] pledged to be married to a man named Joseph, a descendant of David. The virgin's name was Mary. The angel went to her and said, "Greetings, you who are highly favoured! The Lord is with you." Mary was greatly troubled at his words and wondered what kind of greeting this might be. But the angel said to her, "Do not be afraid, Mary, you have found favour with God. You will be with child and give birth to a son, and you are to give him the name Jesus. He will be great and will be called the Son of the Most High. The Lord God will give him the throne of his father David, and he will reign over the house of Jacob forever; his kingdom will never end." "How

[9]The word used here *(alma),* can be distinguished from *b*ᵉ*tûlâ,* used many times in the OT specifically of a virgin. The sense of *alma* is that of a young woman of marriageable age, one of whose characteristics is virginity. There is no instance in the OT where *alma* refers to a young woman who is not a virgin. According to Mt 1:22–23 this text was fulfilled in the virginal conception and birth of Jesus Christ. See *Theological Wordbook of the Old Testament,* eds. Harris, Archer, and Waltke, 2:1630.

[10]*parthenos,* used fourteen times in the NT, always in the sense of "virgin": Mt 1:23, 25:1,7,11; Lk 1:27 (twice); Ac 21:9; 1 Co 7:25,28,34,36,37; 2 Co 11:2; Rev 14:4. Matthew focuses on Joseph's experience, Luke on Mary's.

will this be," Mary asked the angel, "since I am a virgin?" The angel answered, "The Holy Spirit will come upon you, and the power of the Most High will overshadow you. So the holy one to be born will be called the Son of God. Even Elizabeth your relative is going to have a child in her old age, and she who was said to be barren is in her sixth month. For nothing is impossible with God." "I am the Lord's servant," Mary answered. "May it be to me as you have said." Then the angel left her.

Sinlessness

Jesus Christ, conceived by the Holy Spirit, was born without a sinful nature, and though truly tempted, committed no sin. As the sinless Lamb of God he could offer himself as an unblemished sacrifice to God.

Isa 53:9 He was assigned a grave with the wicked, and with the rich in his death, though he had done no violence, nor was any deceit in his mouth.[11]

Lk 1:35 The angel answered, "The Holy Spirit will come upon you, and the power of the Most High will overshadow you. So the holy one to be born will be called the Son of God."

Jn 8:29,46 "The one who sent me is with me; he has not left me alone, for I always do what pleases him. . . . Can any of you prove me guilty of sin? If I am telling the truth, why don't you believe me?"[12]

Jn 14:30–31 "I will not speak with you much longer, for the prince of this world is coming. He has no hold on me,[13] but the world must learn that I love the Father and that I do exactly what my Father has commanded me."

Ac 3:14 "You disowned the Holy and Righteous One and asked that a murderer be relased to you."[14]

**2Co 5:21* God made him who had no sin to

[11]From the "Suffering Servant" passage, a prophecy fulfilled in Jesus Christ.

[12]Christ challenges the unbelieving Pharisees.

[13]Satan could not accuse Christ of violating the law of God. Cf. 1 Co 15:56, "The sting of death is sin, and the power of sin is the law."

[14]Peter preaches to a crowd at the temple after the healing of the lame beggar.

be sin for us, so that in him we might become the righteousness of God.[15]

Heb 4:15 For we do not have a high priest who is unable to sympathize with our weaknesses, but we have one who has been tempted in every way, just as we are—yet was without sin.

Heb 7:26–28 Such a high priest meets our need—one who is holy, blameless, pure, set apart from sinners, exalted above the heavens. Unlike the other high priests, he does not need to offer sacrifices day after day, first for his own sins, and then for the sins of the people. He sacrificed for their sins once for all when he offered himself.

Heb 9:14 How much more, then, will the blood of Christ, who through the eternal Spirit offered himself unblemished to God, cleanse our consciences from acts that lead to death, so that we may serve the living God!

1Pe 1:18–19 For you know that it was not with perishable things such as silver or gold that you were redeemed from the empty way of life handed down to you from your forefathers, but with the precious blood of Christ, a lamb without blemish or defect.

1Pe 2:22–23 "He committed no sin, and no deceit was found in his mouth." When they hurled their insults at him, he did not retaliate; when he suffered, he made no threats. Instead, he entrusted himself to him who judges justly.

1Jn 3:4–5 Everyone who sins breaks the law; in fact, sin is lawlessness. But you know that he appeared so that he might take away our sins. And in him is no sin.

[15]Christ, though he had no personal sin, became our sin-bearer in a representative and vicarious sense. God imputed our sins to Christ, and Christ's righteousness to us.

Humanity

The Logos, the eternal Son of God, in the Incarnation assumed a true and entire human nature unto himself. Because our complete humanity was assumed by the Son of God, human nature in all its aspects can experience the benefits of Christ's redemption. Jesus

Christ, sharing a common human nature with his people, is intimately acquainted with their needs.

Mt 4:1–2 Then Jesus was led by the Spirit into the desert to be tempted by the devil. After fasting forty days and forty nights, he was hungry.

Mt 8:23–24 Then he got into the boat and his disciples followed him. Without warning, a furious storm came up on the lake, so that the waves swept over the boat. But Jesus was sleeping.

Lk 2:52 And Jesus grew in wisdom and stature, and in favour with God and men.[16]

Lk 24:39 "Look at my hands and my feet. It is I myself! Touch me and see; a ghost does not have flesh and bones, as you see I have."[17]

Jn 1:14 The Word became flesh and lived for a while among us.[18]

Jn 4:5–6 So he came to a town in Samaria called Sychar, near the plot of ground Jacob had given to his son Joseph. Jacob's well was there, and Jesus, tired as he was from the journey, sat down by the well.

Jn 11:35 Jesus wept.[19]

Jn 19:28 Later, knowing that all was now completed, and so that the Scripture would be fulfilled, Jesus said, "I am thirsty."[20]

Jn 19:34 One of the soldiers pierced Jesus' side with spear, bringing a sudden flow of blood and water.

Ro 1:2–3 The gospel he promised beforehand through his prophets in the Holy Scriptures regarding his Son, who as to his human nature was a descendant of David. . . .

Heb 2:14 Since the children have flesh and blood, he too shared in their humanity so that by his death he might destroy him who holds the power of death—that is, the devil.

Heb 2:17–18 For this reason he had to be

[16]Jesus grew both mentally and physically.

[17]Even after the resurrection, Jesus has real flesh and bones.

[18]Here "flesh" *(sarx)* means complete human nature. The Word assumed a complete human nature without ceasing to be fully divine.

[19]The shortest verse in Scripture. Jesus had real emotions; he was grieved by the death of his friend Lazarus. He also experienced emotions such as compassion (Mt 9:36) and anger (Mt 3:5).

[20]One of the seven "last words" from the cross.

made like his brothers in every way, in order that he might become a merciful and faithful high priest in service to God, and that he might make atonement for the sins of the people. Because he himself suffered when he was tempted, he is able to help those who are being tempted.

**Heb 4:15* For we do not have a high priest who is unable to sympathize with our weaknesses, but we have one who has been tempted in every way, just as we are—yet was without sin.

Deity

The deity of Jesus Christ in Scripture is demonstrated with reference to divine titles, divine attributes, divine actions, and New Testament texts that specifically state an equality or identity between God and Christ.

DIVINE TITLES

1. "Mighty God"

Isa 9:6 For to us a child is born, to us a son is given, and the government will be on his shoulders. And he will be called Wonderful Counsellor, Mighty God,[21] Everlasting Father, Prince of Peace.
Lord *(kurios):* used in a unique sense by New Testament writers who take Old Testament texts referring to God (Yahweh Adonai) and apply them to Jesus, see E. Eckman, *Gordon Review* 7:4 (1964):145–53.

Mk 1:2–3 It is written in Isaiah[22] the prophet: "I will send my messenger ahead of you, who will prepare your way"—"a voice of one calling in the desert, 'Prepare the way for the Lord, make straight paths for him.' " [Isaiah 40:3, where "Lord" is clearly a reference to God: A voice of one calling: "In the desert prepare the way for the Lord; make straight in the wilderness a highway for our God."]

Lk 1:17 "And he [John the Baptist] will go on before the Lord [Christ], in the spirit and

[21]Notice that elsewhere in Isaiah, e.g., 10:21 "Mighty God" (Hebrew *El gibbor*) clearly refers to God, and not merely to a human messiah: "A remnant will return, a remnant of Jacob will return to the Mighty God."

[22]The quotation in Mk 1:2 is a conflation of Mal 3:1 and Is 40:3. Mark assigns the combined quotation to the more well-known prophet.

power of Elijah . . . to make ready a people prepared for the Lord." [Malachi 3:1, "See, I will send my messenger, who will prepare the way before me. . ."; 4:5, "I will send you the prophet Elijah before that great and dreadful day of the Lord (God) comes."]

Ac 2:21 " 'And everyone who calls on the name of the Lord [here, Jesus] will be saved.' " [Joel 2:32, "And everyone who calls on the name of the Lord (God) will be saved. . . ."]

2. *"Son of God" in a unique sense*

Mt 26:63–65 The high priest said to him, "I charge you under oath by the living God: Tell us if you are the Christ, the Son of God." "Yes, it is as you say," Jesus replied. "But I say to all of you: In the future you will see the Son of Man sitting at the right hand of the Mighty One and coming on the clouds of heaven." Then the high priest tore his clothes and said, "He has spoken blasphemy! Why do we need any more witnesses?"[23]

DIVINE ATTRIBUTES OR QUALITIES

1. *Eternity, pre-existence*

Jn 1:1 In the beginning was the Word, and the Word was with God. . . .[24]

Jn 17:5 [Jesus' priestly prayer]: "And now, Father, glorify me in your presence with the glory I had with you before the world began."

Php 2:5–7 Your attitude should be the same as that of Christ Jesus: Who being in very nature God, did not consider equality with God something to be grasped, but made himself nothing, taking the very nature of a servant, being made in human likeness.

Rev 22:13 [the Risen Christ speaking]: "I am the Alpha and the Omega, the First and the Last, the Beginning and the End."[25]

[23] The reference to the "Son of Man" in v.64 is from Da 7:13, a heavenly, divine being: "In my vision at night I looked, and there before me was one like a son of man, coming with the clouds of heaven." The high priest correctly concluded that Jesus, by assuming the titles of Son of God and Son of Man in this context, was claiming divine status for himself. The synoptic parallel to Mt 26:63–65 is found in Mk 14:61–64.

[24] "In the beginning" does not imply that the Word (Jesus Christ) was created in time, rather, in the beginning, when the divine creative process commenced, the Word already was.

[25] The three contrasts (Alpha-Omega; First-Last; Beginning-End) clearly express Christ's superhuman transcendence over time.

2. Not limited by space[26]

Mt 28:20 "And surely I will be with you always, to the very end of the age."

Eph 1:22–23 . . . the church, which is his body, the fulness of him who fills everything in every way.

3. Universal Power and Authority

Mt 28:18 Then Jesus came to them and said, "All authority in heaven and on earth has been given to me."

Eph 1:22 And God placed all things under his feet and appointed him to be head over everything for the church.

4. Has Life in Himself

Jn 1:4 In him [the Word, Christ] was life, and that life was the light of men.

Jn 5:26 "For as the Father has life in himself, so he has granted the Son to have life in himself."

[26]The risen Christ, while in heaven at the right hand of the Father, is fully present in a spiritual way with the church.

DIVINE ACTIONS AND PREROGATIVES

1. Active in Creation of the World

Jn 1:3 Through him all things were made; without him nothing was made that has been made.

Col 1:16 For by him all things were created: things in heaven and on earth, visible and invisible, whether thrones or powers or rulers or authorities; all things were created by him and for him.

Heb 1:2 In these last days he has spoken to us by his Son, whom he appointed heir of all things, and through whom he made the universe.

2. Sustains the Universe

Col 1:17 He is before all things, and in him all things hold together.

3. *Authority to Forgive Sins*

Mk 2:5–7 When Jesus saw their faith, he said to the paralytic, "Son, your sins are forgiven." Now some teachers of the law were sitting there, thinking to themselves, "Why does this fellow talk like that: He's blaspheming! Who can forgive sins but God alone?"[27]

4. *Object of Prayer*

Ac 7:59 While they were stoning him, Stephen prayed, "Lord Jesus, receive my spirit."

5. *Object of Worship*[28]

Mt 28·16–17 Then the eleven disciples went to Galilee, to the mountain where Jesus had told them to go. When they saw him, they worshipped him; but some doubted.

Jn 20:28 Thomas said to him, "My Lord and my God!"

6. *Power to Raise the Dead*

Jn 5:21 "For just as the Father raises the dead and gives them life, even so the Son gives life to whom he is pleased to give it."

Jn 11:25 Jesus said to her [Martha], "I am the resurrection and the life."

7. *Final Judge of Mankind*

Mt 25:31–32 "When the Son of Man comes in his glory, and all the angels with him, he will sit on his throne in heavenly glory. All the nations will be gathered before him, and he will separate the people one from another as a shepherd separates the sheep from the goats."

Jn 5:22–27 "Moreover, the Father judges no one, but has entrusted all judgment to the son. . . . And he [Father] has given him [Son] authority to judge because he is the Son of Man."[29]

[27]The teachers of the law were correct in their assumption that only God had the authority to forgive sins.

[28]In neither instance does Jesus give any indication that such acts of adoration are inappropriate. Contrast Ac 14:11–15, where Paul and Barnabas refuse religious veneration from the crowds in Lystra and Derbe, and Rev 19:9,10 where the angel refuses worship from John.

[29]As in Mt 26:64, the term Son of Man is very likely Jesus' own self-identification with the heavenly being of Da 7:13.

[30]The Jews sensed that Jesus was here claiming more than unity of purpose with God, and was in fact claiming for himself equality of status with God.

[31]Or, "subsisting in the form of God" (*en morphē theou huparchōn*). "In his preexistent state Christ already had as his possession the unique dignity of His place within the Godhead" (R. P. Martin, Commentary on *Philippians*).

[32]"Greek has two words for 'live' or 'have your home.' The weaker one suggests that your abode is temporary; you may move on. He does not use this word, *paroikein,* but the much stronger word, *katoikein,* which means to 'make your permanent abode.'' The fulness of deity has its permant location in Jesus." Michael

NEW TESTAMENT TEXTS ON EQUALITY OR IDENTITY OF CHRIST AND GOD

1. *Equality*

Jn 10:29–31 "My Father, who has given them to me, is greater than all; no one can snatch them out of my Father's hand. I and the Father are one." Again the Jews picked up stones to stone him. . . .[30]

Jn 14:8–9 Philip said, "Lord, show us the Father and that will be enough for us." Jesus answered: "Don't you know me, Philip, even after I have been among you such a long time? Anyone who has seen me has seen the Father."

Php 2:5–6 Your attitude should be the same as that of Christ Jesus: Who, being in very nature God, did not consider equality with God something to be grasped. . . .[31]

Col 2:9 For in Christ all the fulness of the Deity lives in bodily form.[32]

2. *Identity*

Jn 1:1 In the beginning was the Word, and the Word was with God, and the Word was God.[33]

Jn 20:28 Thomas said to him, "My Lord and my God!"

Tit 2:13 While we wait for the blessed hope—the glorious appearing of our great God and Saviour, Jesus Christ.[34]

Heb 1:8 But about the Son he says, "Your throne, O God, will last for ever and ever."[35]

2Pe 1:1 Simon Peter, a servant and apostle of Jesus Christ, to those who through the righteousness of our God and Saviour Jesus Christ have received a faith as precious as ours.[36]

Green, *The Truth of God Incarnate,* p. 21.

[33]Jehovah's Witnesses attempt to argue that because God *(theos)* in the last clause lacks the definite article *(kai theos . . .),* the translation should read, "and the Word was *a* god," thus denying the full deity of Christ and his equality with the Father. According to the usage of the Greek New Testament, a definite predicative nominative (here, *theos*) has the article when it follows the verb; it does not have the article when it precedes the verb. The correct translation is thus, "and the Word was God." See Bruce Metzger, "The Jehovah's Witnesses and Jesus Christ," *Theology Today* 10 (1953): 65–85, for a thorough discussion.

[34]*tou megalou theou kai sōtēros hēmōn Christou Iēsou:* the absence of the definite article before *sōtēros* indicates that the "great God" and "our Saviour" both refer to the same person, Jesus Christ.

[35]The quotation is from the Septuagint translation of Ps 45:6. The Septuagint was the Greek translation of the Old Testament commonly used in New Testament times. Here the writer of Hebrews ascribes the reference to God's throne to Jesus, the Son.

[36]Here the phrase "our God and Saviour Jesus Christ" is almost identical to that in Titus 2:13, and the same grammatical considerations apply. See note 14 above.

FOR FURTHER READING

Person of Christ

BONSALL, B. *The Person of Christ, Vol. 1: The Doctrine* (1967), 159pp. (A)
CULLMANN, O. *The Christology of the New Testament* (1959), 342pp. (B)
LIDDON, H. P. *The Divinity of our Lord* (1866), many rep. 584pp. (B)
NEILL, S. *The supremacy of Jesus* (1984), 174pp. (B)
WARFIELD, B. B. *The Lord of glory* (1907), 303pp. (B)

7

WORK OF CHRIST

"We could not rejoice that there is a God, were there not a Mediator also; one who stands between God and men, to reconcile man to God, and to transact the whole affair of our salvation" (John Wesley, Notes on 1 Tim. 2:5).

"An absolute God, apart from the Lord Jesus Christ, can afford no comfort whatever to a troubled heart. . . . The only way in which we can see God is through the Mediator Jesus Christ" (Charles H. Spurgeon, Sermon, "Looking Unto Jesus").

Preaching, Teaching, Miracles

By his preaching, teaching, and miracles of healing and exorcism, Jesus gave evidence of his divine mission and the new advent of God's Kingdom in human history.

Mt 4:23–24 Jesus went throughout Galilee, teaching in their synagogues, preaching the good news of the kingdom, and healing every disease and sickness among the people. News about him spread all over Syria, and people brought to him all who were ill with various diseases, those suffering severe pain, the demon-possessed, the epileptics and the paralytics, and he healed them.[1]

Mt 7:28–29 When Jesus had finished saying these things,[2] the crowds were amazed at his teaching, because he taught as one who had authority, and not as their teachers of the law.

[1]Note the distinction made here between demon possession and physical illness. Demon possession may have physical symptoms, but not all illness is related to demonic activity. Cf. also Mk 1:32–34.

[2]The Sermon on the Mount.

Mt 8:16–17 When evening came, many who were demon-possessed were brought to him, and he drove out the spirits with a word and healed all the sick. This was to fulfil what was spoken through the prophet Isaiah: "He took up our infirmities and carried our diseases."[3]

[3]Is 53:4.

Mt 9:35–36 Jesus went through all the towns and villages, teaching in their synagogues, preaching the good news of the kingdom and healing every disease and sickness. When he saw the crowds, he had compassion on them, because they were harassed and helpless, like sheep without a shepherd.[4]

[4]Jesus' healing ministry was an expression of his compassion for the suffering and the lost.

Mk 4:33–34 With many similar parables Jesus spoke the word to them, as much as they could understand. He did not say anything to them without using a parable. But when he was alone with his own disciples, he explained everything.

Lk 9:1–2 When Jesus had called the Twelve together, he gave them power and authority to drive out all demons and to cure diseases, and he sent them out to preach the kingdom of God and to heal the sick.[5]

[5]The disciples were given authority by the Master to preach, to heal, and to cast out demons.

Jn 5:36 "I have testimony weightier than that of John. For the very work that the Father has given me to finish, and which I am doing, testifies that the Father has sent me."[6]

[6]Jesus' miraculous works were evidence of his divine mission.

Jn 12:37 Even after Jesus had done all these miraculous signs in their presence, they still would not believe in him.[7]

[7]The spiritually blind can refuse to see the evidence of God's work for what it truly is.

Jn 20:30–31 Jesus did many other miraculous signs in the presence of his disciples, which are not recorded in this book. But these are written that you may believe that Jesus is the Christ, the Son of God, and that by believing you may have life in his name.[8]

[8]Only a representative selection of Jesus' miracles are recorded in the gospels. The purpose of the accounts is not to promote curiosity, but to promote saving faith in Jesus Christ the Saviour and Lord.

Ac 10:36–38 "This is the message God sent to the people of Israel, telling the good news of peace through Jesus Christ, who is Lord of all. You know what has happened throughout Judea, beginning in Galilee after the baptism that John preached—how God anointed Jesus of Nazareth with the Holy Spirit and power, and how he went around doing good and healing all who were under the power of the devil, because God was with him."[9]

[9]Peter's sermon to Cornelius and his household, recounting the mighty works of Jesus during his earthly ministry.

Obedience of Christ

Jesus' entire life was characterized by obedience. By obeying the will of God completely, even to the point of death, Jesus rendered unto God the perfect obedience to the law, as the Second Adam, which the first Adam had failed to render.

Lk 2:49,51 "Why were you searching for me?" he asked. "Didn't you know I had to be in my Father's house?" . . . Then he went down to Nazareth with them and was obedient to them.[10]

[10]Even though he was the Son of God, the boy Jesus was obedient to his earthly parents.

Jn 6:38 "For I have come down from heaven not to do my will but to do the will of him who sent me."

Jn 8:29 "The one who sent me is with me; he has not left me alone, for I always do what pleases him."

Jn 14:30–31 "He[11] [Satan] has no hold on me, but the world must learn that I love the Father and that I do exactly what my Father has commanded me."

[11]Satan could not accuse Jesus of breaking the law of God.

Jn 15:10 "If you obey my commands, you will remain in my love, just as I have obeyed my Father's commands and remain in his love."

Ro 5:18–19 Consequently, just as the result of one trespass was condemnation for all men, so also the result of one act of righteousness was justification that brings life for all men. For just as through the disobedience of the one man the many were made sinners, so also through the obedience of the one man the many will be made righteous.[12]

[12]The disobedience of Adam brought condemnation to all; the obedience of Christ, culminating in his death on the cross, brings justification to those who believe in him. Paul is not teaching universal salvation here (cf. 2Th 1:8–9 on God's judgment of unbelievers).

Heb 5:8–9: Although he was a son, he learned obedience from what he suffered and, once made perfect, he became the source of eternal salvation for all who obey him.

Php 2:8 And being found in appearance as a man, he humbled himself and became obedient to death—even death on a cross!

Death on the Cross

The Atonement is at the very heart of the Christian faith. Christ died in our place, becoming the object of the wrath of God and the curse of the law, and purchased salvation for all believers. Christ's atoning work was *penal* and *substitutionary* in nature.

Isa 53:4–5 Surely he took up our infirmities and carried our sorrows, yet we considered him stricken by God, smitten by him, and afflicted. But he was pierced for our transgressions, he was crushed for our iniquities; the punishment that brought us peace was upon him, and by his wounds we are healed.[13]

[13]Isaiah's prophecy concerning the Suffering Servant was fulfilled in the death of Christ.

Mk 10:33–34 "We are going up to Jerusalem," he said, "and the Son of Man will be betrayed to the chief priests and teachers of the law. They will condemn him to death and will hand him over to the Gentiles, who will mock him and spit on him, flog him and kill him. Three days later he will rise."[14]

[14]Jesus predicted his own death and resurrection.

Mk 10:45 "For even the Son of Man did not come to be served, but to serve, and to give his life as a ransom for many."

Jn 10:14,15,17,18 "I am the good shepherd . . . I lay down my life for the sheep. . . . The reason my Father loves me is that I lay down my life. . . . No one takes it from me, but I lay it down of my own accord."[15]

[15]Jesus was not a passive victim of circumstances; he freely and consciously chose to die for his people.

Ac 2:23 This man was handed over to you by God's set purpose and foreknowledge; and you, with the help of wicked men, put him to death by nailing him to the cross.[16]

[16]The death of Christ was part of the eternal plan of God.

Ro 3:25 God presented him as a sacrifice of atonement,[17] through faith in his blood.

[17]*hilastērion,* "propitiation," a sacrifice turning aside the wrath of God from the sinner.

Ro 5:10 For if, when we were God's enemies, we were reconciled to him through the death of his Son, how much more, having been reconciled, shall we be saved through his life!

2Co 5:18–19 All this is from God, who reconciled us to himself through Christ and gave us the ministry of reconciliation: that

God was reconciling the world to himself in Christ, not counting men's sins against them.

Gal 3:13 Christ redeemed us from the curse of the law by becoming a curse for us, for it is written: "Cursed is everyone who is hung on a tree."[18]

Eph 2:15–16 His purpose was to create in himself one new man out of the two, thus making peace, and in this one body to reconcile both of them to God through the cross, by which he put to death their hostility.[19]

Eph 5:2 Live a life of love, just as Christ loved us and gave himself up for us as a fragrant offering and sacrifice to God.[20]

Col 1:19–20 For God was pleased to have all his fulness dwell in him, and through him to reconcile to himself all things, whether things on earth or things in heaven, by making peace through his blood, shed on the cross.[21]

Col 2:15 And having disarmed the powers and authorities, he made a public spectacle of them, triumphing over them by the cross.[22]

1Ti 2:5–6 For there is one God and one mediator between God and men, the man Christ Jesus, who gave himself as a ransom for all men.

Heb 9:14 How much more, then, will the blood of Christ, who through the eternal Spirit offered himself unblemished to God, cleanse our consciences from acts that lead to death, so that we may serve the living God![23]

1Pe 1:18–19 For you know that it was not with perishable things such as silver or gold that you were redeemed from the empty way of life handed down to you from your forefathers, but with the precious blood of Christ, a lamb without blemish or defect.

1Pe 2:24 He himself bore our sins in his body on the tree, so that we might die to

[18]The penal and substitutionary elements of the cross are both in view here. The quotation is from Dt 27:26.

[19]The death of Christ reconciled both Jews and Gentiles to God, and made possible their reconciliation to one another.

[20]Christ is the fulfilment of the OT sacrificial system.

[21]While the apostle Paul clearly does not teach universal salvation (see 2Th 1:8–10), the death of Christ has, in some sense, an impact upon the entire universe.

[22]The cross is likened to a military battle in which Christ triumphed over the Devil and his forces.

[23]Jesus Christ, the true High Priest, provides a peace of conscience that sacrifices under the Old Covenant could not offer.

sins and live for righteousness; by his wounds you have been healed.[24]

1Jn 2:2 He is the atoning sacrifice[25] for our sins, and not only for ours but also for the sins of the whole world.

Rev 5:9 And they sang a new song: "You are worthy to take the scroll and to open its seals, because you were slain, and with your blood you purchased men for God from every tribe and language and people and nation."[26]

Resurrection and Ascension[27]

The Resurrection was God's vindication of Christ's teaching and earthly ministry, the demonstration that Christ has defeated sin, death, and the Devil. The Ascension enthroned Christ at God's right hand, where he is now directing and empowering the church in its mission with all authority in heaven and earth.

Mt 28:9 Suddenly Jesus met them. "Greetings," he said. They came to him, clasped his feet and worshipped him.[28]

Lk 24:36–39 While they were still talking about this, Jesus himself stood among them and said to them, "Peace be with you." They were startled and frightened, thinking they saw a ghost. He said to them. . . . "Look at my hands and feet. It is I myself! Touch me and see; a ghost does not have flesh and bones, as you see I have."[29]

Lk 24:50–51 When he had led them out to the vicinity of Bethany, he lifted up his hands and blessed them. While he was blessing them, he left them and was taken up into heaven.

Jn 20:19 On the evening of that first day of the week, when the disciples were together, with the doors locked for fear of the Jews, Jesus came and stood among them and said, "Peace be with you!"[30]

Ac 1:1–2 In my former book, Theophilus, I wrote about all that Jesus began to do and to teach until the day he was taken up to heaven. . . .[31]

[24]The language here reflects Isa 53.

[25]*hilasmos,* "propitiation." See also 1Jn 4:10, "This is love: not that we loved God, but that he loved us and sent his Son as an atoning sacrifice *(hilasmon)* for our sins."

[26]The cross of Christ is foundational for world mission: Christ's blood has purchased salvation for people found in all the world's ethnic groups. Christ was the Lamb slain from the foundation of the world (Rev 13:8).

[27]In most textbooks the death and burial of Christ are included as the last step in the "state of humiliation"; the resurrection is the beginning of the "state of exaltation," which will last for all eternity.

[28]The risen Christ accepts worship from his disciples.

[29]Though Jesus' resurrection body was a glorified body (cf. 1Co 15:42–44), it was nevertheless a real body that could be seen and touched.

[30]Jesus' resurrection body, though a true body, was not subject to some of the normal physical limitations.

[31]In Luke's gospel he described the beginning of Jesus' ministry: the resurrected and ascended Christ is now actively *continuing* his work through the ministry and mission of the

Ac 1:9–11 After he said this, he was taken up before their very eyes, and a cloud hid him from their sight. They were looking intently up into the sky as he was going, when suddenly two men dressed in white stood beside them. "Men of Galilee," they said, "why do you stand here looking into the sky? This same Jesus, who has been taken from you into heaven, will come back in the same way you have seen him go into heaven."[32]

2:32–33 "God has raised this Jesus to life, and we are all witnesses of the fact. Exalted to the right hand of God, he has received from the Father the promised Holy Spirit and has poured out what you now see and hear."[33]

Ro 1:2–4 . . . the gospel he promised beforehand through his prophets in the Holy Scriptures regarding his Son, who as to his human nature was a descendant of David, and who through the Spirit of holiness was declared with power to be the Son of God by his resurrection from the dead: Jesus Christ our Lord.[34]

1Co 15:3–6 For what I received I passed on to you as of first importance: that Christ died for our sins according to the Scriptures, that he was buried, that he was raised on the third day according to the Scriptures, and that he appeared to Peter, and then to the Twelve. After that, he appeared to more than five hundred of the brothers at the same time, most of whom are still living, though some have fallen asleep.[35]

1Co 15:17,20 And if Christ has not been raised, your faith is futile; you are still in your sins. . . . But Christ has indeed been raised from the dead, the firstfruits of those who have fallen asleep.[36]

Eph 1:19–21 That power is like the working of his mighty strength, which he exerted in Christ when he raised him from the dead and seated him at his right hand in the heavenly realms, far above all rule and authority, power and dominion, and every

church. "Theophilus" may be a specific individual, or a generalized term for any "lover of God" who might read the book.

[32]Just as Jesus was raised and taken up into heaven with a physical body, so will he return with a physical body.

[33]Peter's preaching of the resurrection is based on eyewitness testimony. The outpouring of the Spirit is the confirmation of the fact that Jesus is now enthroned in heaven, and is giving spiritual gifts to his people.

[34]The resurrection is God's powerful affirmation of the divine sonship of Jesus Christ and the truth of the gospel.

[35]The resurrection of Christ was one of the core doctrines of the early Christian preaching (*kerygma*). At the time of Paul's writing (c. A.D. 55), hundreds of eyewitnesses to the resurrection were still alive.

[36]The *religious* fact (forgiveness) is based on the *historical* fact (resurrection). These two are inseparable in the apostle's mind—unlike the case in many modern theologies, e.g. Bultmann's. Jesus' resurrection is the inauguration of a new age which will be culminated at the return of Christ and the resurrection of believers.

title that can be given, not only in the present age but also in the one to come.[37]

Php 2:9–11 Therefore God exalted him to the highest place and gave him the name that is above every name, that at the name of Jesus every knee should bow, in heaven and on earth and under the earth, and every tongue confess that Jesus Christ is Lord, to the glory of God the Father.[38]

Heb 4:14 Therefore, since we have a great high priest who has gone through the heavens, Jesus the Son of God, let us hold firmly to the faith we profess.

Heb 7:26 Such a high priest meets our need—one who is holy, blameless, pure, set apart from sinners, exalted above the heavens.[39]

Rev 1:5 . . . Jesus Christ, who is the faithful witness, the firstborn from the dead, and the ruler of the kings of the earth.[40]

[37]Paul prays that the church will experience and apply in its mission the same mighty power of God that raised Jesus from the dead.

[38]Paul quotes an early Christian hymn. The life of Jesus provides an ethical model for believers: obedience and humble service lead to later exaltation and honour.

[39]One reason that the high priesthood of Christ is superior to that of the Old Testament priesthood is that Christ, unlike Aaron, is *exalted above the heavens.*

[40]Words of encouragement to a persecuted church: the believers are, like Christ, to be *faithful witnesses* to the gospel, knowing that Jesus Christ, not Caesar or any earthly king, is Lord, and that not even death or martyrdom can destroy the resurrection message.

FOR FURTHER READING

Work of Christ

art. "The New Testament terminology of redemption" by B. B. Warfield in *Princeton Theol. Rev.* (1917), pp.201–249. Reprinted in *Works,* vol. 2 (1983 reprint) (B)

CRAWFORD, T. J. *The doctrine of Holy Scripture respecting the Atonement* (1874), 538pp. (B)

DENNEY, J. *The death of Christ* (1902) Rev. ed. 1951. 207pp. (B)

MORRIS, L. *The cross in the New Testament* (1965), 454pp. (A)

MORRIS, L. *The Atonement* (1983), 219pp. (B)

MARSHALL, I. H. *The work of Christ* (1969), 128pp. (A)

8

SALVATION AND THE CHRISTIAN LIFE

The death of Christ on the cross for sinners is an objective fact of history. This historic fact is translated into individual Christian experience through the work of the Holy Spirit in initiating the new life in Christ (calling, regeneration, repentance, faith, justification) and perfecting it (sanctification, perseverance).

"In this way you are to become acquainted with the Holy Spirit. You may know to what purpose he is given and what his office is, namely, to invest the treasure—Christ and all he has, who is given to us and proclaimed by the Gospel; the Holy Spirit will give him into your heart so that he may be your own" (Martin Luther, Gospel Sermon, Pentecost Sunday).

Calling and Regeneration

God invites all people everywhere to repent, to believe in Jesus Christ, and to accept the offer of forgiveness and salvation in the gospel. The Holy Spirit implants a new nature in the sinner (regeneration, the new birth), bringing him from darkness into light and from spiritual death into spiritual life.

Isa 45:22 "Turn to me and be saved, all you ends of the earth; for I am God, and there is no other."

Isa 55:1,6–7 "Come, all you who are thirsty, come to the waters; and you who have no money, come, buy and eat! . . ." Seek the Lord while he may be found; call on him while he is near. Let the wicked forsake his way and the evil man his thoughts. Let him turn to the Lord, and he will have mercy on him, and to our God, for he will freely pardon.

Mt 28:19 "Therefore go and make disciples of all nations, baptizing them in the name of the Father and of the Son and of the Holy Spirit. . . ."

Jn 1:12–13 Yet to all who received him, to those who believed in his name, he gave the right to become children of God—children born not of natural descent, nor of human decision or a husband's will, but born of God.[1]

[1]The new birth is not a human accomplishment, but a supernatural work of God.

Jn 3:5–7 Jesus answered, "I tell you the truth, unless a man is born of water and the Spirit, he cannot enter the kingdom of God. Flesh gives birth to flesh, but the Spirit gives birth to spirit. You should not be surprised at my saying, 'You must be born again.' "[2]

[2]The old sinful nature must be changed before man can stand in the presence of God.

Ac 16:14 One of those listening was a woman named Lydia, a dealer in purple cloth from the city of Thyatira, who was a worshipper of God. The Lord opened her heart to respond to Paul's message.[3]

[3]Lydia's conversion in Philippi. The term "regeneration" is not used, but her conversion presupposes it.

Ro 10:14 How, then, can they call on the one they have not believed in? And how can they believe in the one of whom they have not heard? And how can they hear without someone preaching to them.?[4]

[4]Conscious faith in Christ depends upon the preaching of Christ—hence the urgency of evangelism and missions.

Ro 11:28–29 As far as the gospel is concerned, they [the Jews] are enemies on your account; but as far as election is concerned, they are loved on account of the patriarchs, for God's gifts and his call are irrevocable.[5]

[5]God still purposes to call Jews to salvation, on the basis of his covenant with Abraham.

1Co 1:9 God, who has called you into fellowship with his Son Jesus Christ our Lord, is faithful.

1Co 1:23–24 We preach Christ crucified: a stumbling block to Jews and foolishness to Gentiles, but to those whom God has called,[6] both Jews and Greeks, Christ the power of God and the wisdom of God.

[6]A distinction is sometimes made between the *external* calling to all who hear and the *inward* or *effectual* calling (as here) to those who actually repent and believe (the elect).

Eph 2:4–5 But because of his great love for us, God, who is rich in mercy, made us alive with Christ even when we were dead in transgressions—it is by grace you have been saved.[7]

1Ti 6:12 Fight the good fight of faith. Take hold of the eternal life to which you were called when you made your good confession in the presence of many witnesses.

Tit 3:5 . . . he saved us, not because of righteous things we had done, but because of his mercy. He saved us through the washing of rebirth and renewal by the Holy Spirit. . . .[8]

Ja 1:18 He chose to give us birth through the word of truth, that we might be a kind of firstfruits of all he created.

1Pe 1:23 For you have been born again, not of perishable seed, but of imperishable, through the living and enduring word of God.[9]

Rev 22:17 The Spirit and the bride say, "Come!" And let him who hears say, "Come!" Whoever is thirsty, let him come; and whoever wishes, let him take the free gift of the water of life.[10]

[7]The reality of renegeration is presupposed here.

[8]This text is sometimes used to argue that water baptism is the instrument of regeneration. Water baptism, however, is the outward symbol of a spiritual reality that is completely under God's sovereign control. Some, like the thief on the cross (Lk 23:43), enter the kingdom through faith in Christ apart from any water baptism.

[9]The thought is parallel in Jn 1:13. The gospel is the normal means of the Spirit's regenerating work.

[10]Whosoever will may come. The language reflects Isa 55:1.

Repentance and Faith

A new relationship to God is established through repentance and saving faith in Jesus Christ. True repentance involves a frank acknowledgement of sin, sorrow for it, and a determination to forsake the sin. True saving faith involves a commitment of the whole person to Jesus Christ as Lord and Saviour in response to the free offer of salvation in the gospel.

2Ch 7:14 "If my people, who are called by my name, will humble themselves and pray and seek my face and turn from their wicked ways, then I will hear from heaven and will forgive their sin and will heal their land."[11]

Pr 28:13 He who conceals his sins does not prosper, but whoever confesses and renounces them finds mercy.

Isa 55:6–7 "Seek the Lord while he may be found; call on him while he is near. Let the wicked forsake his way and the evil man his

[11]God's promise spoken to Solomon at the dedication of the temple.

thoughts. Let him turn to the Lord, and he will have mercy on him, and to our God, for he will freely pardon."

Eze 18:31–32 "Rid yourselves of all the offences you have committed, and get a new heart and a new spirit. Why will you die, O house of Israel? For I take no pleasure in the death of anyone, declares the Sovereign Lord. Repent and live!"

Joel 2:12–13 "Even now," declares the Lord, "return to me with all your heart, with fasting and weeping and mourning." Rend your heart and not your garments. Return to the Lord your God, for he is gracious and compassionate, slow to anger and abounding in love, and he relents from sending calamity.

Mt 3:1–2 In those days John the Baptist came, preaching in the Desert of Judea and saying, "Repent, for the kingdom of heaven is near."

Mt 4:12,17 When Jesus heard that John had been put in prison, he returned to Galilee. . . . From that time on Jesus began to preach, "Repent for the kingdom of heaven is near."[12]

Lk 24:47–48 "Repentance and forgivness of sins will be preached in his name to all nations, beginning at Jerusalem. You are witnesses of these things."[13]

Ac 2:38 Peter replied, "Repent and be baptized every one of you, in the name of Jesus Christ so that your sins may be forgiven. And you will receive the gift of the Holy Spirit."[14]

Ro 3:28 For we maintain that a man is justified by faith apart from observing the law.

**Ro 5:1* Therefore, since we have been justified through faith, we have peace with God through our Lord Jesus Christ.

Ro 10:17 Consequently, faith comes from hearing the message, and the message is heard through the word of Christ.[15]

[12]Jesus, like John the Baptist before him, stressed repentance as the essential prerequisite for entering the kingdom.

[13]The Lucan form of the Great Commission.

[14]Peter's Pentecost sermon. Note that the gift of the Spirit is promised as an integral part of the salvation experience, rather than something entirely separate from it. Later Christian evangelism has often failed to stress this connection.

[15]Saving faith has a *definite content,* i.e., the gospel message of Christ. Faith involves the emotions, but is founded on objective facts: the life, death, and resurrection of Jesus Christ.

1Co 15:17 And if Christ has not been raised, your faith is futile; you are still in your sins.[16]

Gal 2:20 I have been crucified with Christ and I no longer live, but Christ lives in me. The life I live in the body, I live by faith in the Son of God, who loved me and gave himself for me.[17]

**Eph 2:8–9* For it is by grace you have been saved, through faith—and this is not from yourselves, it is the gift of God—not by works, so that no one can boast.[18]

Heb 11:6 And without faith it is impossible to please God, because anyone who comes to him must believe that he exists and that he rewards those who earnestly seek him.

Ja 2:17–18 In the same way, faith by itself, if it is not accompanied by action, is dead. . . . Show me your faith without deeds, and I will show you my faith by what I do.[19]

1Jn 1:9 If we confess our sins, he is faithful and just and will forgive us our sins and purify us from all unrighteousness.

[16]The apostle unequivocally states that true saving faith is based on the fact of Jesus' resurrection.

[17]True faith touches not merely the "religious" part of our lives, but permeates our entire existence.

[18]The basis of our salvation is grace; faith is the instrument through which we receive it. This faith should not be misconstrued as a form of "spiritual works."

[19]Paul emphasizes that no one earns salvation by works (Ro 3:28); James emphasizes that faith, if it is genuine, demonstrates itself in action. With this Paul agrees: "The only thing that counts is faith expressing itself through love" (Gal 5:6).

Justification

"Justification is an act of God's free grace, wherein he pardons all our sins, and accepts us as righteous in his sight, only for the righteousness of Christ imputed to us, and received by faith alone" (*West. Shorter Catechism,* q. 33).

Ps 32:1–2 Blessed is he whose transgressions are forgiven, whose sins are covered. Blessed is the man whose sin the Lord does not count against him and in whose spirit is no deceit.[20]

Isa 53:11 . . . by his knowledge my righteous servant will justify many, and he will bear their iniquities.[21]

Lk 18:14 "I tell you that this man [the tax collector], rather than the other [the Pharisee], went home justified before God. For everyone who exalts himself will be

[20]Quoted in Ro 4:6, in relation to justification.

[21]The merits of Christ, the Suffering Servant, are imputed to believers.

humbled, and he who humbles himself will be exalted."[22]

Ac 13:39 "Through him everyone who believes is justified from everything you could not be justified from by the law of Moses."[23]

Ro 3:20 Therefore no one will be declared righteous in his sight by observing the law; rather, through the law we become conscious of sin.

**Ro 3:23–24* For all have sinned and fall short of the glory of God, and are justified freely by his grace through the redemption that came by Christ Jesus.

Ro 3:28 For we maintain that a man is justified by faith apart from observing the law.

**Ro 5:1* Therefore, since we have been justified through faith, we have peace with God through our Lord Jesus Christ.

1Co 6:11 You were washed, you were sanctified, you were justified in the name of our Lord Jesus Christ and by the Spirit of our God.

Gal 2:16 So we, too, have put our faith in Christ Jesus that we may be justified by faith in Christ and not by observing the law, because by observing the law no one will be justified.

Gal 3:24 The law was put in charge to lead us to Christ that we might be justified by faith.

Tit 3:5,7 He saved us through the washing of rebirth and renewal by the Holy Spirit . . . so that, having been justified by his grace, we might become heirs having the hope of eternal life.

Jas 2:21–22 Was not our ancestor Abraham considered righteous for what he did when he offered his son Isaac on the altar? You see that his faith and his actions were working together, and his faith was made complete by what he did.[24]

[22]This parable of Jesus exemplifies the principle of justification through faith.

[23]Paul's sermon in the synagogue at Pisidian Antioch.

[24]There is no contradiction here to the apostle Paul's teaching. "The only thing that counts is faith expressing itself through love" (Gal 5:6). True saving faith expresses itself in love and obedience. "Every good tree bears good fruit (Mt 7:17).

Sanctification

The Christian's growth in holiness and conformity to the character of Jesus Christ through personal faith and obedience and the ministry of the Holy Spirit and the Word of God. Some Christian traditions understand sanctification in terms of crisis experiences leading to Christian perfection (Holiness, Pentecostal, Nazarene); others understand sanctification primarily in terms of a continuous process which never reaches a state of Christian perfection in this life (Reformed, Lutheran, Anglican).

WESLEYAN VIEW

("Christian perfection" or "entire sanctification"): in this view, the state of holiness begins at regeneration and is completed by an instantaneous work of the Holy Spirit [the baptism of the Holy Spirit] subsequent to regeneration, in which the old Adamic sin nature is actually abolished. "Christian perfection . . . is nothing more and nothing less than a heart emptied of all sin and filled with a pure love to God and man" (Wiley, 2:511).[25]

Ge 6:9 Noah was a righteous man, blameless among the people of his time, and he walked with God.

Ge 17:1 When Abram was ninety-nine years old, the Lord appeared to him and said, "I am God Almighty; walk before me and be blameless."

Job 1:1 In the land of Uz there lived a man whose name was Job. This man was blameless and upright; he feared God and shunned evil.[26]

Mt 5:48 "Be perfect, therefore, as your heavenly Father is perfect."

Mk 12:28–30 One of the teachers of the law came and heard them debating. Noticing that Jesus had given them a good answer, he asked him, "Of all the commandments, which is the most important?" "The most important one," answered Jesus, "is this:

[25]The baptism of the Holy Spirit may include, but is not necessarily identified with the outward manifestation of speaking in tongues (though some in this tradition would make this identification). "Christian perfection" is not absolute moral perfection or perfection in knowledge, but a state in which the believer is freed from the power of sin, sin understood as a voluntary transgression of a known law of God.

[26]Even in the Old Covenant, prior to the fulness of the Spirit's work, individuals such as Noah and Job are specifically commended for their personal sanctity.

'Hear, O Israel, the Lord our God, the Lord is one. Love the Lord your God with all your heart and with all your soul and with all your mind and with all your strength.' "[27]

[27]Ge 17:1, Mt 5:48, Mk 12:30: God sets the highest possible spiritual standards for the lives of his people.

Ac 15:8–9 "God, who knows the heart, showed that he accepted them [the Gentiles] by giving the Holy Spirit to them, just as he did to us. He made no distinction between us and them, for he purified[28] their hearts by faith."

[28]*katharisas,* aorist participle of *katharizō,* purify.

2Co 7:1 Since we have these promises, dear friends, let us purify ourselves from everything that contaminates body and spirit, perfecting holiness out of reverence for God.[29]

[29]An apostolic admonition for the post-conversion state.

Gal 5:24 Those who belong to Christ Jesus have crucified[30] the sinful nature with its passions and desires.

[30]*estaurōsan,* aorist of *staurōo,* crucify.

Eph 1:13 And you also were included in Christ when you heard the word of truth, the gospel of your salvation. Having believed, you were marked[31] in him with a seal, the promised Holy Spirit.

[31]*esphragisthēte,* aorist passive of *sphragizō,* seal. It is argued that the aorist tenses in Ac 15:9, Gal 5:24, and Eph 1:13 point to the definitive, punctilear nature of the Spirit's work in sanctification.

1Th 5:23 May God himself, the God of peace, sanctify you through and through. May your whole spirit, soul and body be kept blameless at the coming of our Lord Jesus Christ.

Heb 6:1 Therefore let us leave the elementary teachings about Christ and go on to maturity,[32] not laying again the foundation of repentance from acts that lead to death. . . .

[32]Or "perfection," KJV *(teleistēta).*

REFORMED VIEW

In this view, the state of holiness begins with regeneration and conversion, and is to grow throughout the believer's life through the ministry of the Word and Spirit and through personal faith and obedience. In this understanding, the old sin nature is progressively subdued, but never entirely abolished in this life. In justification, sin is pardoned; in sanctification it is subdued. Sanctification ". . . is neither equal in all, nor in this life perfect in any, but growing up to perfection" (*West. Larger Catechism,* q. 77).

1Ki 8:46,49,50 "When they sin against you—for there is no one who does not sin . . . then from heaven . . . hear their prayer. . . . And forgive your people."[33]

Mt 6:12 " 'Forgive us our debts, as we have also forgiven our debtors.' "[34]

Lk 9:23 Then he [Jesus] said to them all: "If anyone would come after me, he must deny himself and take up his cross daily and follow me."[35]

Ro 8:1–2 Therefore, there is now no condemnation for those who are in Christ Jesus, because through Christ Jesus the law of the Spirit of life set me free from the law of sin and death.[36]

Eph 5:18 Do not get drunk on wine, which leads to debauchery. Instead, be filled[37] with the Spirit.

Php 3:12 Not that I have already obtained all this,[38] or have already been made perfect, but I press on to take hold of that for which Christ Jesus took hold of me.

Jas 3:2 We all stumble in many ways. If anyone is never at fault in what he says, he is a perfect man, able to keep his whole body in check.

1Jn 1:8–9 If we claim to be without sin, we deceive ourselves and the truth is not in us. If we confess our sins, he is faithful and just and will forgive us our sins and purify us from all unrighteousness.[39]

[33]From Solomon's prayer of dedication for the temple.

[34]Believers still stand in need of forgiveness.

[35]Death to sin and self is to be the daily experience of the believer.

[36]No believer need live a life defeated by sin.

[37]*plērousthe:* present passive imperative, "keep on being filled with the Spirit." The infilling of the Spirit is to be continuous and progressive in the believer's experience.

[38]"This" refers to the power of Christ's resurrection, and the fellowship with Christ in his suffering and death and the final resurrection mentioned in VV. 10–11. The apostle Paul did not consider that he had already been perfected *(ēdē teteleiōma)* in these things.

[39]John writes to those who have made some Christian profession, who have made some "claim to have fellowship with him" (v. 6), yet who may be living inconsistently with that profession.

PENTECOSTAL DISTINCTIVES: THE BAPTISM IN THE HOLY SPIRIT

"This wonderful experience is distinct from and subsequent to the experience of the new birth . . . the baptism of believers in the Holy Ghost is witnessed by the initial physical signs of speaking with other tongues as the Spirit of God gives them utterance." Articles Seven and Eight, "Statement of Fundamental Truths," 35th General Council of the Assemblies of God, August 16–21, 1973.

Mt 3:11 "I baptize you with water for repentance. But after me will come one who is more powerful than I, whose sandals I am not fit to carry. He will baptize you with the Holy Spirit and with fire."

Mk 1:8 "I baptize you with water, but he will baptize you with the Holy Spirit."

[*Mk 16:17* "And these signs will accompany those who believe: In my name they will drive out demons; they will speak in new tongues. . . ."][40]

Lk 3:16 John answered them all, "I baptize you with water. But one more powerful than I will come, the thongs of whose sandals I am not worthy to untie. He will baptize you with the Holy Spirit and with fire."[41]

Ac 1:4–5 On one occasion, while he was eating with them, he gave them this command: "Do not leave Jerusalem, but wait for the gift my Father promised, which you have heard me speak about. For John baptized with water, but in a few days you will be baptized with the Holy Spirit."

Ac 2:1–4 When the day of Pentecost came, they were all together in one place. Suddenly a sound like the blowing of a violent wind came from heaven and filled the whole house where they were sitting. They saw what seemed to be tongues of fire that separated and came to rest on each of them. All of them were filled with the Holy Spirit and began to speak in other tongues as the Spirit enabled them.[42]

Ac 8:14–17 When the apostles in Jerusalem heard that Samaria had accepted the word of God, they sent Peter and John to them. When they arrived, they prayed for them that they might receive the Holy Spirit, because the Holy Spirit had not yet come

[40]Mark 16:9–20 is not contained in the earliest manuscripts.

[41]John the Baptist points to Jesus the Baptizer in the Holy Spirit. John's words were fulfilled on the Day of Pentecost.

[42]These events were a fulfilment of the prophecy of Joel, Joel 2:28–32.

upon any of them; they had simply been baptized into the name of the Lord Jesus. Then Peter and John placed their hands on them, and they received the Holy Spirit.[43]

Ac 10:44–46 While Peter was still speaking these words [to Cornelius and his household], the Holy Spirit came on all who heard the message. The circumcised believers who had come with Peter were astonished that the gift of the Holy Spirit had been poured out even on the Gentiles. For they heard them speaking in tongues and praising God.[44]

Ac 19:1–6 While Apollos was at Corinth, Paul took the road through the interior and arrived at Ephesus. There he found some disciples and asked them, "Did you receive the Holy Spirit when you believed?" They answered, "No, we have not even heard that there is a Holy Spirit." So Paul asked, "Then what baptism did you receive?" "John's baptism," they replied. Paul said, "John's baptism was a baptism of repentance. He told the people to believe in the one coming after him, that is, in Jesus." On hearing this, they were baptized into the name of the Lord Jesus. When Paul placed his hands on them, the Holy Spirit came on them, and they spoke in tongues and prophesied.[45]

1Co 12:7–11 Now to each one the manifestation of the Spirit is given for the common good. To one there is given through the Spirit the message of wisdom, to another the message of knowledge by means of the same Spirit, to another faith by the same Spirit, to another gifts of healing by that one Spirit, to another miraculous powers, to another prophecy, to another the ability to distinguish between spirits, to another the ability to speak in different kinds of tongues, and to still another the interpretation of tongues. All these are the work of one and the same Spirit, and he gives them to each one, just as he determines.

1Co 12:13 For we were all baptized by one

[43]The Samaritan believers had experienced no outward evidence of the giving of the Holy Spirit prior to the arrival of Peter and John.

[44]In this case the manifestation of tongues helped convince the Jewish believers that God was in fact extending salvation to the Gentiles.

[45]Some interpreters see these disciples as imperfectly instructed believers. In the light of v.3, however, it appears more likely that they were not yet Christians, but only disciples of John the Baptist.

Spirit into one body—whether Jews or Greeks, slave or free—and we were all given the one Spirit to drink.[46]

[46]The verse can also be translated "with one Spirit" or "in one Spirit." In light of v.11, it would appear that the Spirit is the active agent, hence favouring the rendering "by one Spirit."

1Co 14:4–5 He who speaks in a tongue edifies himself, but he who prophesies edifies the church. I would like every one of you to speak in tongues, but I would rather have you prophesy. He who prophesies is greater than one who speaks in tongues, unless he interprets, so that the church may be edified.[47]

[47]Tongues plus interpretation are the functional equivalent of prophecy.

1Co 14:39–40 Therefore, my brothers, be eager to prophesy, and do not forbid speaking in tongues. But everything should be done in a fitting and orderly way.

Perseverance

There are differences of opinion within Evangelical circles on the question of whether a truly regenerate person can irreversibly fall away from the faith and be ultimately lost. Those of a Reformed or Calvinistic persuasion believe that the elect persevere, demonstrating their election, and by the grace of God cannot fall away. Those who hold a Wesleyan or Arminian perspective believe that apostasy is a real possibility for a true believer.

REFORMED VIEW

Jn 6:37,39 "All that the Father gives me will come to me, and whoever comes to me I will never drive away. . . . And this is the will of him who sent me, that I shall lose none of all that he has given me, but raise them up at the last day."

Jn 10:28–29 "I give them eternal life, and they shall never perish; no one can snatch them out of my hand. My father, who has given them to me, is greater than all; no one can snatch them out of my Father's hand."

Jn 17:11–12 "I will remain in the world no longer, but they are still in the world, and I am coming to you. Holy Father, protect them by the power of your name—the name you gave me—so that they may be one as we are one."

Ro 8:30 And those he predestined, he also called; those he called, he also justified; those he justified, he also glorified.[48]

Ro 8:38–39 For I am convinced that neither death nor life, neither angels nor demons, neither the present nor the future, nor any powers, neither height nor depth, nor anything else in all creation, will be able to separate us from the love of God that is in Christ Jesus our Lord.

**Php 1:6* Being confident of this, that he who began a good work in you will carry it on to completion until the day of Christ Jesus.

2Ti 1:2 . . . I know whom I have believed, and am convinced that he is able to guard what I have entrusted to him for that day.

2Ti 2:13 If we are faithless, he will remain faithful, for he cannot disown himself.

2Ti 4:18 The Lord will rescue me from every evil attack and will bring me safely to his heavenly kingdom.

**1Jn 5:13* I write these things to you who believe in the name of the Son of God so that you may know[49] that you have eternal life.

WESLEYAN/ARMINIAN VIEW

Mt 13:20–21 "What was sown on rocky places is the man who hears the word and at once receives it with joy. But since he has no root, he lasts only a short time. When trouble or persecution comes because of the word, he quickly falls away."[50]

Jn 15:6 If anyone does not remain in me, he is like a branch that is thrown away and withers; such branches are picked up, thrown into the fire and burned.

Ro 11:22 Consider therefore the kindness and sternness of God: sternness to those who fell, but kindness to you, provided that you continue in his kindness. Otherwise, you also will be cut off.

[48] God will bring those he truly predestines, calls, and justifies safely into heavenly glory.

[49] *eidētē:* second perfect active subjunctive of *oida,* "to know with settled intuitive knowledge" (A. T. Robertson). John is writing in order that believers might have firm assurance of their salvation.

[50] Parable of the sower. In this interpretation, the saying refers to a regenerate person who later falls away.

Col 1:22–23 But now he has reconciled you by Christ's physical body through death to present you holy in his sight, without blemish and free from accusation—if you continue in your faith, established and firm, not moved from the hope held out in the gospel.[51]

[51]Christian growth and sanctification are not an automatic process.

1Ti 1:19–20 Some have rejected these [faith and a good conscience] and so have shipwrecked their faith. Among them are Hymenaeus and Alexander, whom I have handed over to Satan[52] to be taught not to blaspheme.

[52]This may refer to excommunication from the church. By being placed outside of the church, one is thrust from the kingdom of light into the kingdom of darkness (cf. Col 1:13).

2Ti 2:12 If we endure, we will also reign with him. If we disown him, he will also disown us.

2Ti 4:10 Demas, because he loved this world, has deserted me and has gone to Thessalonica.

Heb 3:14 We have come to share in Christ if we hold firmly till the end the confidence we had at first.

Heb 6:4–6 It is impossible for those who have once been enlightened,[53] who have tasted the heavenly gift, who have shared in the Holy Spirit, who have tasted the goodness of the word of God and the powers of the coming age, if they fall away, to be brought back to repentance, because to their loss they are crucifying the Son of God all over again and subjecting him to public disgrace.

[53]It is argued that the word, translated "enlightened" *(phōtisthentas,* from *phōtizō)* must refer to a believer, since it is evidently used in this sense in 10:32: "Remember those earlier days after you had received the light (*phōtisthentes*), when you stood your ground in a great contest in the face of suffering."

2Pe 2:1, 20–21 But there were also false prophets among the people, just as there will be false teachers among you. . . . If they have escaped the corruption of the world by knowing our Lord and Savior Jesus Christ and are again entangled in it and overcome, they are worse off at the end than they were at the beginning. It would have been better for them not to have known the way of righteousness, than to have known it and then to turn their backs on the sacred commandment that was passed on to them.

FOR FURTHER READING

Salvation and Christian Life

GREEN, E. M. B. *The meaning of salvation* (1965), 256pp. (B)
HAMMOND, T. C. *The new creation* (1953), 192pp. (A)
MOULE, H. C. G. *Faith, its nature and work* (1909), 240pp. (A)
BONHOEFFER, D. *The cost of discipleship* (1959), 285pp. (B)

Repentance and faith

IRONSIDE, H. A. *Except ye repent* (1937), 191pp. (A)
MACHEN, J. G. *What is faith?* (1925), 262pp. (B)

Calling and regeneration

art. "Call, calling" by R. Mackintosh, in Hastings' *Dictionary of Christ and the Gospels*, I, 264–66. (A)

Justification

BUCHANAN, J. *Doctrine of Justification* (1867), rep. 1961. 524pp. (B)
STOTT, J. R. W. *Men made new* (1966), 108pp. (A)

Sanctification

BERKOUWER, G. C. *Faith and sanctification* (1952), 192pp. (C)
LLOYD-JONES, D. M. *Life in the Spirit* (1974), 371pp. (B)
MARSHALL, W. *The Gospel mystery of sanctification* (1692) many rep. (B)
MURRAY, A. *Holy in Christ* (1888), 302pp. (A)
RYLE, J. C. *Holiness* (1879), rep. 1952, 333pp. (A)

Perseverance

LLOYD-JONES, D. M. *Romans 8:17–39: The final perseverance of the saints* (1975), 457pp.

9

THE CHURCH

"I believe that there is on earth, through the whole wide world, no more than one holy, common, Christian Church, which is nothing else than the congregation, or assembly of the saints, i.e., the pious, believing men on earth, which is gathered, preserved, and ruled by the Holy Ghost, and daily increased by means of the sacraments and the Word of God" (Martin Luther, "A Brief Explanation of the Ten Commandments, the Creed, and the Lord's Prayer.").

Nature of the Church

BIBLICAL NAMES AND DESCRIPTIONS

Ro 9:25–26 As he says in Hosea: "I will call them 'my people' who are not my people; and I will call her 'my loved one' who is not my loved one," and, "It will happen that in the very place where it was said to them, 'You are not my people,' they will be called 'sons of the living God.' "[1]

Ro 12:4–5 Just as each of us has one body with many members, and these members do not all have the same function, so in Christ we who are many form one body, and each member belongs to all the others.

1Co 3:9 For we are God's fellow workers; you are God's field, God's building.

1Co 3:16–17 Don't you know that you yourselves are God's temple and that God's Spirit lives in you? If anyone destroys God's

[1]The quotations are from Hos 2:23 and Hos 1:10. The church is designated as the "people of God."

temple, God will destroy him; for God's temple is sacred, and you are that temple.[2]

1Co 12:12–13 The body is a unit, though it is made up of many parts; and though all its parts are many, they form one body. So it is with Christ. For we were all baptized by one Spirit into one body—whether Jews or Greeks, slave or free—and we were all given the one Spirit to drink.

Gal 4:26 But the Jerusalem that is above is free, and she is our mother.[3]

Gal 6:16 Peace and mercy to all who follow this rule, even to the Israel of God.[4]

Eph 2:14–16 For he himself is our peace, who has made the two one and has destroyed the barrier, the dividing wall of hostility, by abolishing in his flesh the law with its commandments and regulations. His purpose was to create in himself one new man out of the two, thus making peace, and in this one body to reconcile both of them to God through the cross by which he put to death their hostility.[5]

Eph 2:19–20 Consequently, you are no longer foreigners and aliens, but fellow citizens with God's people and members of God's household, built on the foundation of the apostles and prophets, with Christ Jesus himself as the chief cornerstone.

Eph 4:15–16 Speaking the truth in love, we will in all things grow up into him who is the Head, that is, Christ. From him the whole body, joined and held together by every supporting ligament, grows and builds itself up in love, as each part does its work.

Eph 5:23 For the husband is the head of the wife as Christ is the head of the church, his body, of which he is the Saviour.[6]

1Ti 3:14–15 Although I hope to come to you soon, I am writing you these instructions so that, if I am delayed, you will know how people ought to conduct themselves in God's household, which is the church of the

[2]God's temple (*naos*) is no longer a physical building, but his people among whom his Spirit dwells.

[3]The church is the spiritual Jerusalem, and the mother of the faithful. It should be noted, though, that dispensationalists would deny that this verse makes such an identification. See also note 4 below.

[4]The apostle calls the one church of Jew and Gentile the "Israel of God." However, dispensationalists understand the church to be a new entity that came into existence at Pentecost (Mt 16:18, cf. Ac 2 and Eph 3:2–6). Consequently, dispensationalists do not understand the church to be a "spiritual Israel" or the "Israel of God." They point out that "Israel of God" in 6:16 could be referring to either Jewish believers in the church or to believing national Israel as distinct from the church.

[5]God has created the church as the new humanity, ending the former hostility of Jew and Gentile through the cross.

[6]In the NT the church is described as the bride of Christ, as Israel in the OT was spoken of as the bride of Yahweh (e.g. Hos 2).

living God, the pillar and foundation of the truth.

Heb 12:22–23 But you have come to Mount Zion, to the heavenly Jerusalem, the city of the living God. You have come to thousands upon thousands of angels in joyful assembly, to the church of the firstborn, whose names are written in heaven.

1Pe 2:4–5 As you come to him, the living Stone—rejected by men but chosen by God and precious to him—you also, like living stones, are being built into a spiritual house to be a holy priesthood, offering spiritual sacrifices acceptable to God through Jesus Christ.[7]

[7]The NT church is the successor to the OT temple; NT believers are the spiritual successors of the Levitical priesthood.

Rev 21:2 I saw the Holy City, the new Jerusalem, coming down out of heaven from God, prepared as a bride beautifully dressed for her husband.

ATTRIBUTES OF THE CHURCH

The church in the New Testament is characterized by unity, holiness, and catholicity. The church as the body of Christ is spritually one in him; as the temple of the Holy Spirit, it is holy in his sight; it is "catholic" in the sense of being universal, being limited to no one culture, race, or ethnic group, but intended for the entire world.

Mt 28:19 "Therefore go and make disciples of all nations, baptizing them in the name of the Father and of the Son and of the Holy Spirit."

Ro 12:4–5 Just as each of us has one body with many members, and these members do not all have the same function, so in Christ we who are many form one body, and each member belongs to all the others.

1Co 12:12 The body is a unit, though it is made up of many parts; and though all its parts are many, they form one body. So it is with Christ.

Gal 3:26–28 You are all sons of God through faith in Christ Jesus, for all of you who were baptized into Christ have clothed yourselves with Christ. There is neither Jew nor Greek, slave nor free, male nor female, for you are all one in Christ Jesus.[8]

Eph 4:4–6 There is one body and one Spirit—just as you were called to one hope when you were called—one Lord, one faith, one baptism; one God and Father of all, who is over all and through all and in all.[9]

Eph 5:25–27 Husbands, love your wives, just as Christ loved the Church and gave himself up for her to make her holy, cleansing her by the washing with water through the word, and to present her to himself as a radiant church, without stain or wrinkle or any other blemish, but holy and blameless.

Col 1:6 All over the world this gospel is producing fruit and growing, just as it has been doing among you since the day you heard it and understood God's grace in all its truth.

1Th 4:3,7 It is God's will that you should be holy; that you should avoid sexual immorality. . . . For God did not call us to be impure, but to live a holy life.

Tit 2:13–14 . . . our great God and Saviour, Jesus Christ, who gave himself for us to redeem us from all wickedness and to purify for himself a people that are his very own, eager to do what is good.

1Pe 2:5 You also, like living stones, are being built into a spiritual house to be a holy priesthood, offering spiritual sacrifices acceptable to God through Jesus Christ.

Rev 7:9 After this I looked and there before me was a great multitude that no one could count, from every nation, tribe, people and language, standing before the throne and in front of the Lamb.[10]

[8] Salvation in Christ transcends worldly divisions based on race, social class, or gender.

[9] If Paul uses the metaphor of the body to describe local congregations in Ro 12 and 1Co 12, here his attention seems to be focused on the unity of the church universal.

[10] A spendid vision of the catholicity or universality of the church at the conclusion of history. John foresees the time when the Great Commission will have been completed with phenomenal success.

Government of the Church

Although all Christians, as members of the body of Christ, have various ministries of service, the New Testament provides for the offices of elder (or bishop) and deacon to give continuing leadership to the church.

GENERAL TEXTS

Ac 6:1–6 In those days when the number of disciples was increasing, the Grecian Jews among them complained against those of the Aramaic-speaking community because their widows were being overlooked in the daily distribution of food. So the Twelve gathered all the disciples together and said, "It would not be right for us to neglect the ministry of the word of God in order to wait on tables. Brothers, choose seven men from among you who are known to be full of the Spirit and wisdom. We will turn this responsibility over to them and will give our attention to prayer and the ministry of the word." This proposal pleased the whole group. They chose Stephen, a man full of faith and of the Holy Spirit; also Philip, Procorus, Nicanor, Timon, Parmenas, and Nicolas from Antioch, a convert to Judaism. They presented these men to the apostles, who prayed and laid their hands on them.[11]

1Th 5:12–13 Now we ask you, brothers, to respect those who work hard among you, who are over you in the Lord and who admonish you. Hold them in the highest regard in love because of their work. Live in peace with each other.[12]

1Ti 3:1–13 Here is a trustworthy saying: If anyone sets his heart on being an overseer, he desires a noble task. Now the overseer must be above reproach, the husband of but one wife, temperate, self-controlled, respectable, hospitable, able to teach, not given to much wine, not violent but gentle, not quarrelsome, not a lover of money. He must manage his own family well and see that his children obey him with proper respect. (If anyone does not know how to manage his

[11]Generally considered to be a description of the first deacons. The Greek-speaking widows were being neglected; the seven men chosen were all from a Hellenistic background, as their names indicate. The apostles recognized the wisdom of bringing into leadership positions men from ethnic backgrounds other than their own.

[12]Evidently there were continuing church officers in Thessalonica, though the offices are not specifically named. Many scholars consider the letters to the Thessalonians to be among the earliest of Paul's epistles. This corresponds to the picture presented in the Book of Acts, where from the beginning of his ministry Paul is concerned to appoint leaders in the churches.

own family, how can he take care of God's church?) He must not be a recent convert, or he may become conceited and fall under the same judgment as the devil. He must also have a good reputation with outsiders, so that he will not fall into disgrace and into the devil's trap.[13]

Deacons, likewise, are to be men worthy of respect, sincere, not indulging in much wine, and not pursuing dishonest gain. They must keep hold of the deep truths of the faith with a clear conscience. They must first be tested; and then if there is nothing against them, let them serve as deacons. In the same way, their wives[14] are to be women worthy of respect, not malicious talkers but temperate and trustworthy in everything. A deacon must be the husband of but one wife and must manage his children and his household well. Those who have served well gain an excellent standing and great assurance in their faith in Christ Jesus.

Tit 1:6–9 An elder must be blameless, the husband of but one wife, a man whose children believe and are not open to the charge of being wild and disobedient. Since an overseer is entrusted with God' work, he must be blameless—not overbearing, not quick-tempered, not given to much wine, not violent, not pursuing dishonest gain. Rather he must be hospitable, one who loves what is good, who is self-controlled, upright, holy and disciplined. He must hold firmly to the trustworthy message as it has been taught, so that he can encourage others by sound doctrine and refute those who oppose it.

Heb 13:7 Remember your leaders, who spoke the word of God to you. Consider the outcome of their way of life and imitate their faith.

1Pe 5:1–4 To the elders among you, I appeal as a fellow elder, a witness of Christ's sufferings and one who also will share in the glory to be revealed: Be shepherds of God's flock that is under your care, serving

[13]The qualifications of the overseer or elder are primarily those of character, not formal education or social position. The elder's home and family life (vv. 4–5) should provide a good example for the congregation.

[14]This could possibly be a reference to "deaconesses" rather than to the wives of deacons.

as overseers—not because you must, but because you are willing, as God wants you to be; not greedy for money, but eager to serve; not lording it over those entrusted to you, but being examples to the flock. And when the Chief Shepherd apears, you will receive the crown of glory that will never fade away.

CONGREGATIONAL CHURCH GOVERNMENT

In this form of church government, found in Congregational, Baptist, and Independent churches, the local congregation is not subject in a binding way to other church councils or denominational agencies. The local church ordains ministers, and through its elected officers, exercises the power of church discipline. "While Christ is sole King . . . the government of the church, so far as regards the interpretation and execution of his will by the body, is an absolute democracy, in which the whole body of members is intrusted with the duty and responsibility of carrying out the law of Christ as expressed in his word" (A. H. Strong, *Systematic Theology,* p. 903).

Mt 18:17 "If he refuses to listen to them, tell it to the church; and if he refuses to listen even to the church, treat him as you would a pagan or a tax collector."[15]

Ac 6:3,5 "Brothers, choose seven men from among you who are known to be full of the spirit and wisdom. . . ." This proposal pleased the whole group. . . .[16]

2Co 2:6–7 The punishment inflicted on him by the majority is sufficient for him. Now instead, you ought to forgive and comfort him, so that he will not be overwhelmed by excessive sorrow.[17]

2Co 8:19 What is more, he [the "brother" of v.18] was chosen by the churches to accompany us as we carry the offering, which we administer in order to honour the

[15]Notice that the entire church is involved in the disciplinary process at this point.

[16]The apostles did not simply appoint the deacons at their own initiative; the deacons were chosen by the people.

[17]Again, the entire congregation is involved in the discipline of the offender. Cf. also 2Th 3:14–15.

Lord himself and to show our eagerness to help.[18]

2Th 3:14–15 If anyone does not obey our instruction in this letter, take special note of him. Do not associate with him, in order that he may feel ashamed. Yet do not regard him as an enemy, but warn him as a brother.

Jude 3 Dear friends, although I was very eager to write to you about the salvation we share, I felt I had to write and urge you to contend for the faith that was once for all entrusted to the saints.[19]

[18]The "brother" (not named by Paul) who was to accompany the collection for the poor in Jerusalem was appointed to this task by the churches.

[19]Jude admonishes all the believers to be concerned for the preservation of the apostolic doctrine.

PRESBYTERIAN CHURCH GOVERNMENT

"It is expedient and agreeable to Scripture and to the practice of the early Christians that the Church be governed by representative assemblies, composed of Presbyters or Elders. These assemblies, called Church courts, in the order of their regular gradation, are: Church Sessions, Presbyteries, Synods, and the General Assembly" (*The Book of Church Order*, Presbyterian Church U.S., 1982–83, par. 13–1). This form of government is found in Reformed and Presbyterian churches and, in a modified form, in American Lutheran churches.

Ac 15:1,6,22,23,28–29 Some men came down from Judea to Antioch and were teaching the brothers: "Unless you are circumcised, according to the custom taught by Moses, you cannot be saved. . . ." The apostles and elders met to consider this question. . . . Then the apostles and elders, with the whole church, decided to choose some of their own men and send them to Antioch with Paul and Barnabas. . . . With them they sent the following letter: ". . . It seemed good to the Holy Spirit and to us not to burden you with anything beyond the following requirements: You are to abstain from food sacrificed to idols, from blood, from the meat of strangled animals and from sexual immorality. You will do well to avoid these things."[20]

Ac 20:17,28 From Miletus, Paul sent to Ephesus for the elders of the church. . . . "Keep watch over yourselves and all the flock of which the Holy Spirit has made you overseers. Be shepherds of the church of God, which he bought with his own blood."[21]

Eph 4:4,16 There is one body and one Spirit—just as you were called to one hope-when you were called. . . . From him [Christ] the whole body, joined and held together by every supporting ligament, grows and builds itself up in love, as each part does its work.[22]

1Ti 4:14 Do not neglect your gift, which was given you through a prophetic message when the body of elders laid their hands on you.[23]

Jas 5:14 Is any one of you sick? He should call the elders of the church to pray over him and anoint him with oil in the name of the Lord.[24]

EPISCOPAL CHURCH GOVERNMENT

In this ecclesiastical tradition the power of ordination and spiritual oversight over the churches in a certain district (diocese) are vested in the bishop. The episcopal form of government is found in the Roman Catholic, Eastern Orthodox, Anglican, Episcopalian and, in modified form, in the Methodist and European Lutheran communions. An episcopal form of government is literally government by bishops: the Greek word *episkopos* is the word normally translated in English as "bishop" or "overseer."

"The evidence is in favour of the supposition that Episcopacy sprang from the Church itself, and by a natural process, and that it was sanctioned by S. John, the last survivor of the Apostles.

[20]As a result of a dispute over whether or not the Gentile converts should be circumcised, the apostles and elders of the church in Jerusalem send a pastoral letter to the church in Antioch. Here is an example in the New Testament of leaders in one church exercising spiritual authority over another church. However, Congregationalists point out that the whole church was involved from begining to end (15:22,30).

[21]The elders have special responsibilities for the oversight of the church beyond those of the ordinary church member.

[22]Here Paul speaks of the unity of the church universal. The individual believers and congregation are not seen as isolated units, but as part of a larger spiritual organism with Christ as the head.

[23]Timothy received his ordination through the laying on of hands of the council of elders. Paul was evidently a member of this ordaining group (cf. 2Ti 1:6, "I remind you to fan into flame the gift of God, which is in you through the laying on of my hands").

[24]According to James, the elders are to have a special role in the ministry of healing through prayer.

. . . Thus it is probable that at an early period an informal episcopate had sprung up in each church" (E. A. Litton, *Introduction to Dogmatic Theology on the Basis of the Thirty-Nine Articles,* p. 393).

Mt 16:18–19 "And I tell you that you are Peter, and on this rock I will build my church, and the gates of Hades will not overcome it. I will give you the keys of the kingdom of heaven; whatever you bind on earth will be bound in heaven, and whatever you loose on earth will be loosed in heaven."[25]

Ac 14:21–23 They preached the good news in that city [Derbe] and won a large number of disciples. Then they returned to Lystra, Iconium and Antioch, strengthening the disciples and encouraging them to remain true to the faith. . . . Paul and Barnabas appointed elders for them in each church and, with prayer and fasting, committed them to the Lord in whom they had put their trust.[26]

Php 1:1 Paul and Timothy, servants of Christ Jesus, To all the saints in Christ Jesus at Philippi, together with the overseers [or, "bishops"] and deacons.

1Ti 3:1 Here is a trustworthy saying: If anyone sets his heart on being an overseer [or "bishop"], he desires a noble task.

2Ti 1:6 For this reason I remind you to fan into flame the gift of God, which is in you through the laying on of my hands.[27]

Tit 1:5 The reason I left you in Crete was that you might straighten out what was left unfinished and appoint elders in every town, as I directed you.[28]

[25]The Roman Catholic Church points to these verses as the foundation of the papacy. Note, however, that nothing whatsoever is mentioned here concerning a *succession* of "bishops" following Peter. And in John 20:22–23, the "power of the keys" is given not just to Peter, but to all the disciples.

[26]Here Paul and Barnabas appoint leaders in the churches; no mention is made of elections by the congregations.

[27]It might be suggested that here Paul's action in the ordination of Timothy is analogous to the ordination of a priest by a modern bishop.

[28]As in Acts 14:21–23, here too elders are to be appointed for the churches, in this case by Titus, the apostle Paul's personal representative.

Mission of the Church

The mission of the church is carried out through evangelism, foreign missions, acts of benevolence and social compassion, discipleship training and Christian nurture. Through these varied activities the kingdom of God is extended both in the world and in the hearts of believers.

Mt 28:18–20 Then Jesus came to them and said, "All authority in heaven and on earth has been given to me. Therefore go and make disciples of all nations,[29] baptizing them in the name of the Father and of the Son and of the Holy Spirit, and teaching them to obey everything I have commanded you. And surely I will be with you always, to the very end of the age."

Mk 16:15–16 He said to them, "Go into all the world and preach the good news to all creation. Whoever believes and is baptized will be saved, but whoever does not believe will be condemned.[30]

Lk 24:45–49 Then he opened their minds so they could understand the Scriptures. He told them, "This is what is written: The Christ will suffer and rise from the dead on the third day, and repentance and forgiveness of sins will be preached in his name to all nations, beginning at Jerusalem. You are witnesses of these things. I am going to send you what my Father has promised; but stay in the city until you have been clothed with power from on high."

Jn 20:21–22 Again Jesus said, "Peace be with you! As the Father has sent me, I am sending you." And with that he breathed on them and said, "Receive the Holy Spirit."

Ac 1:7–8 He said to them: "It is not for you to know the times or dates the Father has set by his own authority. But you will receive power when the Holy Spirit comes on you; and you will be my witnesses in Jerusalem, and in all Judea and Samaria, and to the ends of the earth."[31]

Ro 12:6–8 We have different gifts, according to the grace given us. If a man's gift is prophesying, let him use it in proportion to his faith. If it is serving, let him serve; if it is teaching, let him teach; it if is encouraging, let him encourage; if it is contributing to the needs of others, let him give generously; if

[29]The Greek term translated "nations," *ta ethnē,* could better be rendered as "ethnic groups"—as a reminder that existing maps of nation-states (i.e., *political* boundaries) do not adequately represent the richness of the mosaic of ethnic groups around the globe. The Great Commission will not have been fulfilled until there are disciples from *every* tongue and tribe and nation (Rev 7:9).

[30]The earliest Greek manuscripts of the Gospel of Mark do not include vv. 9–20.

[31]It is noteworthy that the Great Commission appears in all four gospels and in the Book of Acts; a clear indication of its importance.

it is leadership, let him govern diligently; if it is showing mercy, let him do it cheerfully.[32]

1Co 16:1–3 Now about the collection for God's people: Do what I told the Galatian churches to do. On the first day of every week, each one of you should set aside a sum of money in keeping with his income, saving it up, so that when I come no collections will have to be made. Then, when I arrive, I will give letters of introduction to the men you approve and send them with your gift to Jerusalem.[33]

Gal 6:10 Therefore, as we have opportunity, let us do good to all people, especially to those who belong to the family of believers.[34]

Eph 4:11–13 It was he [Christ] who gave some to be apostles, some to be prophets, some to be evangelists, and some to be pastors and teachers, to prepare God's people for works of service, so that the body of Christ may be built up until we all reach unity in the faith and in the knowledge of the Son of God and become mature, attaining to the whole measure of the fulness of Christ.[35]

1Ti 4:13 Until I come, devote yourself to the public reading of Scripture, to preaching and to teaching.[36]

1Ti 5:3–4,16 Give proper recognition to those widows who are really in need. But if a widow has children or grandchildren, these should learn first of all to put their religion into practice by caring for their own family and so repaying their parents and grandparents, for this is pleasing to God. . . . If any woman who is a believer has widows in her family, she should help them and not let the church be burdened with them, so that the church can help those widows who are really in need.[37]

2Ti 4:2 Preach the Word; be prepared in season and out of season; correct, rebuke

[32]The success of the mission of the church depends on the healthy functioning of the various members of the body of Christ.

[33]Paul placed considerable importance on this collection for the impoverished believers in Jerusalem. Two entire chapters (8 and 9) in 2 Corinthians are devoted to this concern. Christian congregations are to share financially with one another in order to meet urgent needs and to demonstrate the sincerity of Christian love. Cf. Jas 2:15–16: "Suppose a brother or sister is without clothes and daily food. If one of you says to him, 'Go, I wish you well; keep warm and well fed,' but does nothing about his physical needs, what good is it?"

[34]There is a clear sense of priorities here for social ministry: First the needs within the Christian community, then the needs of the world.

[35]The ascended Christ gives gifts of ministry to the church not so that "full-time Christian workers" do all the ministry, but in order that the *whole church* be equipped to do the work of ministry.

[36]Paul wants the reading and exposition of Scripture to be central in Timothy's ministry. The word *proseche,* "devote yourself, attend to," is a present active imperative with the sense, "keep on putting your mind on" (A. T. Robertson).

[37]The care of widows was a significant concern in the early church (cf. Ac 6:1–6). Paul teaches that the care of widows was first of all the responsibility of the children and the

and encourage—with great patience and careful instruction.

immediate family, and then of the church. No mention is made of government in this connection.

Tit 3:14 Our people must learn to devote themselves to doing what is good,[38] in order that they may provide for daily necessities and not live unproductive lives.

[38]*kalōn ergōn,* lit., "good works." "Our people must really learn to make themselves practically useful" (Scott). Christians are to be actively engaged in works of practical mercy.

Heb 13:1–3,16 Keep on loving each other as brothers. Do not forget to entertain strangers, for by so doing some people have entertained angels without knowing it. Remember those in prison as if you were their fellow prisoners, and those who are mistreated as if you yourselves were suffering. . . .[39] And do not forget to do good and to share with others, for with such sacrifices God is pleased.

[39]The writer probably has in mind primarily *Christians* who are imprisoned for their faith. Christians are to be known for their hospitality and good works.

Jas 1:27 Religion that God our Father accepts as pure and faultless is this: to look after orphans and widows in their distress and to keep oneself from being polluted by the world.

Jas 5:14–15 Is any one of you sick? He should call the elders of the church to pray over him and anoint him with oil in the name of the Lord. And the prayer offered in faith will make the sick person well; the Lord will raise him up. If he has sinned, he will be forgiven.[40]

[40]In the "non-charismatic" Epistle of James, it is notable that healing is to be a normal part of the ministry of the church.

1Pe 4:9–11 Offer hospitality to one another without grumbling. Each one should use whatever gift he has received to serve others, faithfully administering God's grace in its various forms. If anyone speaks, he should do it as one speaking the very words of God. If anyone serves, he should do it with the strength God provides, so that in all things God may be praised through Jesus Christ.

1Jn 3:16–18 This is how we know what love is: Jesus Christ laid down his life for us. And we ought to lay down our lives for our brothers. If anyone has material possessions and sees his brother in need but has no pity on him, how can the love of God be in him? Dear children, let us not love with words or tongue but with actions and in truth.[41]

[41]The thought here is closely paralleled in Jas 2:14–17. Christian love and faith show themselves in action.

FOR FURTHER READING

The Church

art. "Church" in *New International Dictionary of New Testament Theology* I, 291–305. (B)
BEST, E. *One body in Christ* (1955), 256pp. (C)
HORT, F. J. A. *The Christian ecclesia* (1900), 306pp. (B)
MINEAR, P. *Images of the Church in the New Testament* (1961), 294pp. (B)
NEWBIGIN, L. *The household of God* (1953), 155pp. (B)
WATSON, D. *I believe in the Church* (1978), 368pp. (A)

10

SACRAMENTS

The sacraments are "visible signs of an invisible grace" (Augustine). Baptism and the Lord's Supper were instituted by Christ as continuing signs of our initiation into the visible community of God's people and our enjoyment of the spiritual benefits of his death and resurrection.

"There are, strictly speaking, but two sacraments in the Church of God—baptism and bread; for only in these two do we find both the divinely instituted sign and the promise of the forgiveness of sins" (Martin Luther).

In Baptist and Independent traditions the terminology of "ordinances" rather than "sacraments" is generally preferred. Ordinances are ". . . those outward rites which Christ has appointed to be administered in his church as visible signs of the saving truth of the gospel" (A. H. Strong, *Systematic Theology,* p. 930). The term "sacrament," on the other hand, connotes to some, a "Catholic" understanding of a rite that has power in itself to confer grace on the recipient.

Baptism

Christians differ on the question of the proper mode of baptism. For the view that the New Testament command to baptize is a command to immerse, see A. H. Strong, *Systematic Theology,* pp. 933–40; for the view that baptism may be properly administered by either immersion, pouring, or sprinkling, see Charles Hodge, *Systematic Theology,* 3:526–39.

GENERAL TEXTS

Mt 38:19 "Therefore go and make disciples

of all nations, baptizing them in the name of the Father and of the Son and of the Holy Spirit. . . ."[1]

Ac 2:38–39 Peter replied, "Repent and be baptized, every one of you, in the name of Jesus Christ so that your sins may be forgiven. And you will receive the gift of the Holy Spirit. The promise is for you and for your children and for all who are far off—for all whom the Lord our God will call."[2]

Ro 6:3–5 Don't you know that all of us who were baptized into Christ Jesus were baptized into his death? We were therefore buried with him through baptism into death in order that, just as Christ was raised from the dead through the glory of the Father, we too may live a new life. If we have been united with him in his death, we will certainly also be united with him in his resurrection.[3]

Gal 3:27–28 All of you who were baptized into Christ have clothed yourselves with Christ. There is neither Jew nor Greek, slave nor free, male nor female, for you are all one in Christ Jesus.[4]

Eph 4:4–6 There is one body and one Spirit—just as you were called to one hope when you were called—one Lord, one faith, one baptism; one God and Father of all, who is over all and through all and in all.[5]

Tit 3:5 He saved us, not because of righteous things we had done, but because of his mercy. He saved us through the washing of rebirth and renewal by the Holy Spirit.[6]

BELIEVER'S BAPTISM

According to this understanding of the nature of baptism, only those persons who show personal faith in Jesus Christ should be baptized. Those who hold to this position point to the constant association of faith, repentance, and baptism in the New Testament.

Ac 2:38 Peter replied, "Repent and be baptized, every one of you, in the name of

[1]Even though water baptism is not essential to salvation (cf. Lk 23:43, the thief on the cross), believers should be baptized out of obedience to this command of Christ. The triune nature of God is seen in this baptismal formula.

[2]Peter here connects water baptism and the promise of the gift of the Holy Spirit—two elements which became separated in later church history.

[3]Baptism signifies a spiritual identification with Jesus Christ in his death and resurrection.

[4]Baptism is the outward sign of a spiritual unity that transcends distinctions of race, social class, or gender.

[5]It is one of the ironies and tragedies of church history that baptism, intended to be a symbol of unity among believers, has so frequently become a point of contention and disunity.

[6]In the Roman Catholic, Eastern Orthodox, and "high church" Anglican traditions, it is held that this reference to the "washing of rebirth" (*loutrou palingenesias*) teaches that the recipient of water baptism receives the new birth by this means. This view, known as "baptismal regeneration," is not held by Protestant Evangelicals.

Jesus Christ so that your sins may be forgiven."[7]

Ac 16:14–15 One of those listening was a woman named Lydia, a dealer in purple cloth from the city of Thyatira, who was a worshipper of God. The Lord opened her heart to respond to Paul's message. When she and the members of her household were baptized, she invited us to her home.[8]

Act 16:31–33 They replied [to the Philippian jailer], "Believe in the Lord Jesus, and you will be saved—you and your household." Then they spoke the word of the Lord to him and to all the others in his house. At that hour of the night the jailer took them and washed their wounds; then immediately he and all his family were baptized.

Ac 18:8 Crispus, th synagogue ruler, and his entire household believed in the Lord; and many of the Corinthians who heard him believed and were baptized.

Ro 6:4 We were therefore buried with him through baptism into death in order that, just as Christ was raised from the dead through the glory of the Father, we too may live a new life.[9]

1Pe 3:21 . . . and this water [of the Flood] symbolizes baptism that now saves you also—not the removal of dirt from the body but the pledge of a good conscience toward God.[10]

[7]Repentance and baptism are here tied together.

[8]Lydia expressed personal faith ("The Lord opened her heart to respond . . .") prior to her baptism.

[9]Baptism signifies *newness of life*—which presupposes the presence of living faith.

[10]If baptism represents the appeal of a *good conscience,* this again presupposes the existence of repentance and faith.

INFANT BAPTISM

According to this understanding, not only are adult converts to be baptized, but also the infant children of one or both believing parents. Baptism of the infant is understood as a sign of the covenant, signifying membership in the visible people of God. Baptism in the New Testament replaces circumcision in the Old Testament as the covenant sign. The promise of salvation which it symbolizes is to be personally appropriated, by faith, by the child when the age of accountability is reached. In the Lutheran understanding, it is the faith of the parents which supplies the faith associated with the sign of baptism in the New Testament.

Ge 17:11–13 "You are to undergo circumcision, and it will be the sign of the covenant between me and you. For the generations to come every male among you who is eight days old must be circumcised, including those born in your household or bought with money from a foreigner—those who are not your offspring. Whether born in your household or brought with your money, they must be circumcised. My covenant in your flesh is to be an everlasting covenant."[11]

Lk 18:15–17 People were also bringing babies to Jesus to have him touch them. When the disciples saw this, they rebuked them. But Jesus called the children to him and said, "Let the little children come to me, and do not hinder them, for the kingdom of God belongs to such as these. I tell you the truth, anyone who will not receive the kingdom of God like a little child will never enter it."[12]

Ac 2:39 "The promise is for you and your children and for all who are far off—for all whom the Lord our God will call."[13]

Ac 16:15 When she [Lydia] and the members of her household were baptized, she invited us to her home.[14]

Ac 16:33 At that hour of the night the [Philippian] jailer took them and washed their wounds; then immediately he and all his family were baptized.

1Co 1:16 Yes, I also baptized the household of Stephanas; beyond that, I don't remember if I baptized anyone else.

1Co 7:14 For the unbelieving husband has been sanctified through his wife, and the unbelieving wife has been sanctified through her believing husband. Otherwise your children would be unclean, but as it is, they are holy.[15]

[11]Abraham applied circumcision, the sign of the covenant, to the male members of his household in response to the command of God. The divine command signified God's intent to deal with the family as an organic unit, even though not all members may have at the time expressed personal faith.

[12]Jesus' willingness to touch the infants expressed God's concern for and interest in these covenant children. In praying for the children (Mt 19:13), Jesus invoked the name and blessing of the God of Israel upon them just as in baptism the name of the triune God is invoked upon the person being baptized.

[13]The phrase "you and your children" expresses the common outlook of the Old Testament: God desires to deal with households as households, and not just as an atomistic collection of individuals.

[14]It seems rather likely that in at least one of these household baptisms—here, and in vv.31–33 and 1Co 1:16—some infants or young children were involved.

[15]The spouses and the children in question are not "holy" in the sense of being converted, but in the sense of being "set apart" through their family relationship to a believer. In this sense the households of Noah and Abraham were "sanctified" by the faith of the head of the household. Cf. Paul's language in Ro 11:16, "if the root is holy, so are the branches"—i.e., God still has an interest in the unbelieving Jews of Paul's day (the "branches") because of the promises

Gal 3:14 He redeemed us in order that the blessing given to Abraham might come to the Gentiles through Christ Jesus, so that by faith we might receive the promise of the Spirit.[16]

Col 2:11–12 In him [Christ] you were also circumcised, in the putting off of the sinful nature, not with a circumcision done by the hands of men but with the circumcision done by Christ, having been buried with him in baptism and raised with him through your faith in the power of God, who raised him from the dead.[17]

made to the patriarchs Abraham, Isaac, and Jacob (the "roots").

[16]In this text Paul makes it clear that the Abrahamic covenant, far from being obsolete, provides the spiritual basis for the salvation of the Gentiles. The spiritual meaning of the Abrahamic covenant is not abolished in the New Testament.

[17]In Jesus Christ, the spiritual meaning of circumcision is fulfilled in baptism. Since the NT nowhere teaches that children of believers have fewer privileges than children of believers in the OT, the implication is that children of believers today are entitled to the outward sign of membership in the covenant and the visible body of God's people.

Lord's Supper

The Lord's Supper is a sacrament instituted by Jesus Christ, wherein believers are reminded of his death on the cross, and through faith are spiritually nourished and personally participate in the saving benefits of his atoning death.

GENERAL TEXTS

Ex 12:24–27 "Obey these instructions as a lasting ordinance for you and your descendants. When you enter the land that the Lord will give you as he promised, observe this ceremony. And when your children ask you, 'What does this ceremony mean to you?' then tell them, 'It is the Passover sacrifice to the Lord, who passed over the houses of the Israelites in Egypt and spared our homes when he struck down the Egyptians.' " Then the people bowed down and worshipped.[18]

[18]The OT Passover was a spiritual prefiguring of the NT ordinance of the Lord's Supper.

Mt 26:26–28 While they were eating, Jesus took bread, gave thanks and broke it, and gave it to his disciples, saying, "Take and eat; this is my body." Then he took the cup, gave thanks and offered it to them, saying, "Drink from it, all of you. This my blood of the covenant, which is poured out for many for the forgiveness of sins."[19]

[19]Jesus used the occasion of the Passover meal celebrated with his disciples (v.17) to institute a new Christian observance.

Mk 14:22–24 While they were eating, Jesus broke bread, gave thanks and broke it, and gave it to his disciples, saying, "Take it; this is my body." Then he took the cup, gave thanks and offered it to them, and they all drank from it. "This is my blood of the covenant, which is poured out for many," he said to them.

Lk 22:19–20 And he took bread, gave thanks and broke it, and gave it to them, saying, "This is my body given for you; do this in remembrance of me." In the same way, after supper he took the cup, saying, "This cup is the new covenant in my blood, which is poured out for you."[20]

Jn 6:53–55 Jesus said to them, "I tell you the truth, unless you eat the flesh of the Son of Man and drink his blood, you have no life in you. Whoever eats my flesh and drinks my blood has eternal life, and I will raise him up at the last day. For my flesh is real food and my blood is real drink. Whoever eats my flesh and drinks my blood remains in me, and I in him."[21]

Ac 2:42,46–47 They devoted themselves to the apostles' teaching and to the fellowship, to the breaking of bread and to prayer. . . . Every day they continued to meet together in the temple courts. They broke bread in their homes and ate together with glad and sincere hearts, praising God and enjoying the favour of all the people. And the Lord added to their number daily those who were being saved.

Ac 20:7 On the first day of the week we came together to break bread. Paul spoke to the people and, because he intended to leave the next day, kept on talking until midnight.[22]

1Co 11:23–29 For I received from the Lord what I also passed on to you: The Lord Jesus, on the night he was betrayed, took bread, and when he had given thanks, he broke it and said, "This is my body, which is for you; do this in remembrance of me." In the same way, after supper he took the cup, saying, "This cup is the new covenant in my blood; do this, whenever you drink it, in remembrance of me." For whenever you eat

[20]There are slight variations in the words of institution as reported by Matthew, Mark, Luke, and Paul. The New Testament writers considered it adequate to their purposes to give an accurate paraphrase of the words of Jesus, according to the form of the tradition that had been passed on to them.

[21]Some scholars believe that the "Bread of Life" discourse in chapter 6, especially vv.53–59, represents the Johannine version of the Lord's Supper. The eating of the Passover meal seems to be assumed in chapter 13.

[22]The expression "breaking of bread" here and in 2:42 "probably denotes a fellowship meal in the course of which the Eucharist was celebrated" (F. F. Bruce).

this bread and drink this cup, you proclaim the Lord's death until he comes. Therefore, whoever eats the bread or drinks the cup of the Lord in an unworthy manner will be guilty of sinning against the body and blood of the Lord. A man ought to examine himself before he eats of the bread and drinks of the cup. For anyone who eats and drinks without recognizing the body of the Lord eats and drinks judgment on himself.[23]

LUTHERAN VIEW

According to this understanding, sometimes known as "consubstantiation," the body and blood of Christ are really present "in, with, and under the elements." "It is taught among us that the true body and blood of Christ are really present in the Supper of our Lord under the form of bread and wine and are there distributed and received" (Augsburg Confession, X).

Mt 26:26–28 While they were eating, Jesus took bread, gave thanks and broke it, and gave it to his disciples, saying, "Take and eat; this is my body." Then he took the cup, gave thanks and offered it to them, saying, "Drink from it, all of you. This is my blood of the covenant, which is poured out for many for the forgiveness of sins."[24]

1Co 10:16 Is not the cup of thanksgiving for which we give thanks a participation in the blood of Christ? And is not the bread that we break a participation in the body of Christ?[25]

1Co 11:23–24,29 For I received from the Lord what I also passed on to you: The Lord Jesus, on the night he was betrayed, took bread, and when he had given thanks, he broke it and said, "This is my body, which is for you; do this in remembrance of me. . . ." For anyone who eats and drinks without recognizing the body of the Lord eats and drinks judgment on himself.

REFORMED AND WESLEYAN VIEWS

In these traditions, the body and blood of

[23]These warnings are not intended to frighten sincere believers, but to guard against carnal and careless attitudes when approaching the Lord's Table. Unconfessed sin and unreconciled relationships should be dealt with before coming to God in worship. Cf. Mt 5:23–24: "If you are offering your gift at the altar and there remember that your brother has something against you, leave your gift there in front of the altar. First go and be reconciled to you brother; then come and offer your gift."

[24]In the Lutheran understanding, the clear references to the body and blood of Christ should not be spiritualized away. The bread and wine remain, but the body and blood of Christ are present in a supernatural but very real way.

[25]The word translated here as "participation" is *koinōnia,* which can also mean "sharing, fellowship, or partnership."

Christ, and the saving benefits they represent, are understood to be spiritually present in the elements of the Lord's Supper. "Worthy receivers, outwardly partaking of the visible elements in this sacrament, do then also inwardly by faith, really and indeed, yet not carnally and corporally, but spiritually, receive and feed upon Christ crucified, and all the benefits of his death . . ." (Westminster Confession, XXIX.vii). "The body of Christ is given, taken, and eaten in the Supper only after a heavenly and spiritual manner. And the means whereby the body of Christ is received and eaten in the Supper is faith" ([Methodist] Articles of Religion, XVIII).

Mt 26:26–28 (see above for text)

1Co 10:16[26] (see above for text)

Jn 6:63 The Spirit gives life; the flesh counts for nothing. The words I have spoken to you are spirit and they are life.[27]

ZWINGLIAN VIEW

According to this tradition, associated with the Swiss reformer Huldrych Zwingli (1484–1531), and commonly held in many Baptist and independent churches today, the Lord's Supper is an occasion when the believer recalls and commemorates the death of Christ and its spiritual meaning for the Christian. This is also known as the "memorial" view. In this observance ". . . the members of the church, by use of bread and wine, commemorate the dying love of Christ" (Report of Committee on Baptist Faith and Message, Southern Baptist Convention, 1925, XVIII).

Lk 22:19 And he took bread, gave thanks and broke it, and gave it to them, saying, "This is my body given for you; do this in remembrance of me."[28]

1Co 11:24–25 . . . "This is my body, which is

[26]In this understanding, the reference to the body and blood refers to a spiritual presence; in 1Co 10:16, the participation is a spiritual participation.

[27]In the conclusion to the "Bread of Life" discourse, Jesus points his listeners away from a literal understanding of his references to flesh and blood. His words and the spiritual meaning they convey are the real pathway to eternal life.

[28]In this and the 1Co 11 passage the element of remembrance is an explicit part of the Lord's command. It should be noted that in the Passover meal, which forms the OT background of the Lord's Supper, the people of Israel were to remember God's mighty acts of redemption in delivering them from bondage in Egypt.

for you; do this in remembrance of me." In the same way, after supper, he took the cup, saying, "This cup is the new covenant in my blood; do this, whenever you drink it, in remembrance of me."

FOR FURTHER READING

Sacraments

BERKOUWER, G. C. *The Sacraments* (1969), 304pp. (C)
CANDLISH, J. S. *The Christian sacraments* (Handbooks for Bible classes) (1879). (A)
FORSYTH, P. T. *Church and sacraments* (1917), 309pp. (C)
BRIDGE, D. AND D. PHYPERS *The meal that unites?* (1981), 191pp. (B)
BRIDGE, D. AND D. PHYPERS *The water that divides* (1978), 208pp. (B)

11

INDIVIDUAL ESCHATOLOGY

Eschatology is the study of the biblical teachings concerning the "last things." Individual eschatology examines the phenomenon of death as an individual experience and the question of the intermediate state—the state of the dead in the period between death and the final resurrection.

"Consider! You were not created to please your senses, to gratify your imagination, to gain money, or the praise of men. . . . On the contrary, you were created for this, and for no other purpose, by seeking and finding happiness in God on earth, to secure the glory of God in heaven" (John Wesley, Sermons, "What is Man?" 13,15).

Death

Gen 2:16–17 And the Lord God commanded the man, "You are free to eat from any tree in the garden; but you must not eat from the tree of the knowledge of good and evil, for when you eat of it you will surely die."[1]

Pr 8:35–36 "Whoever finds me [Wisdom] finds life and receives favour from the Lord. But whoever fails to find me harms himself; all who hate me love death."[2]

Ecc 3:1–2 There is a time for everything, and a season for every activity under heaven: a time to be born and a time to die. . . .

Ecc 8:8 No man has power over the wind to contain it; so no one has power over the day of his death.[3]

Ez 18:23 Do I take any pleasure in the death

[1]According to Scripture, death is not merely a biological phenomena, but is a consequence of disobedience to the command of God.

[2]Disregard for God's wisdom revealed in Scripture eventually leads to physical and spiritual death.

[3]The times of our birth and our death are determined by the plan of God.

of the wicked? declares the Sovereign Lord. Rather, am I not pleased when they turn from their ways and live?

Mt 10:28 Do not be afraid of those who kill the body but cannot kill the soul. Rather, be afraid of the one who can destroy both soul and body in hell.[4]

Ro 5:12 Therefore, just as sin entered the world through the one man, and death through sin, and in this way death came to all men, because all sinned. . . .[5]

**Ro 6:23* For the wages of sin is death, but the gift of God is eternal life in Christ Jesus our Lord.

1Co 15:54–57 When the perishable has been clothed with the imperishable, and the mortal with immortality, then the saying that is written will come true: "Death has been swallowed up in victory." "Where, O death, is your victory? Where, O death, is your sting?" The sting of death is sin, and the power of sin is the law. But thanks be to God! He gives us the victory through our Lord Jesus Christ.[6]

2Ti 1:9–10 This grace was given us in Christ Jesus before the beginning of time, but it has now been revealed through the appearing of our Saviour, Christ Jesus, who has destroyed death and has brought life and immortality to light through the gospel.

Heb 2:14–15 Since the children have flesh and blood, he too shared in their humanity so that by his death he might destroy him who holds the power of death—that is, the devil—and free those who all their lives were held in slavery by their fear of death.

Heb 9:27–28 Just as man is destined to die once, and after that to face judgment,[7] so Christ was sacrificed once to take away the sins of many people. . . .

Rev 1:18 I am the Living One; I was dead, and behold I am alive for ever and ever! And I hold the keys of death and Hades.

Rev 21:3–4 And I heard a loud voice from

[4]Earthly persecutors may have the power to destroy the body, but only God has authority over man's eternal destiny.

[5]Adam's sin brought death not only upon himself, but also upon all his descendants.

[6]Death's ultimate defeat has been manifested in the resurrection of Jesus Christ.

[7]This text clearly rules out reincarnation: each human being dies *once,* and then faces the Creator in judgment. Life is not an unending cycle of birth, death, and rebirth.

the throne saying, "Now the dwelling of God is with men, and he will live with them. They will be his people, and God himself will be with them and be their God. He will wipe every tear from their eyes. There will be no more death or mourning or crying or pain, for the old order of things has passed away."

[8]In the Roman Catholic tradition the "prison" is taken as a reference to purgatory. In the context, however, an *earthly* prison is clearly intended in this illustration.

[9]This text, and its parallels in Mk 5:39 and Lk 8:52, have sometimes been taken to teach "soul sleep"—the view that the souls of the dead are not conscious prior to the final resurrection, but sleeping. This language, however, is metaphorical, i.e., sleep is in some respects an illustration of death. Note Jn 11:11,13–14: "Our friend Lazarus has fallen asleep; but I am going there to wake him up.' . . . Jesus had been speaking of his death, but his disciples thought he meant natural sleep. So then he told them plainly, 'Lazarus is dead.' "

Intermediate State

This term refers to the state of the dead during the period subsequent to death and prior to the final resurrection. "The souls of believers are at their death made perfect in holiness, and do immediately pass into glory; and their bodies, being still united to Christ, do rest in their graves till the resurrection" (*Westminster Shorter Catechism,* q. 37).

Mt 5:25–26 "Settle matters quickly with your adversary who is taking you to court . . . you may be thrown into prison. I tell you the truth, you will not get out until you have paid the last penny."[8]

Mt 9:23–24 When Jesus entered the ruler's house and saw the flute players and the noisy crowd, he said, "Go away. The girl is not dead but asleep."[9]

Lk 16:22–23 "The time came when the beggar died and the angels carried him to Abraham's side. The rich man also died and was buried. In hell, where he was in torment, he looked up and saw Abraham far away, with Lazarus by his side."[10]

Lk 23:43 Jesus answered him [the thief on the cross], "I tell you the truth, today you will be with me in paradise."[11]

1Co 3:12–15 If any man builds on this foundation using gold, silver, costly stones, wood, hay or straw, his work will be shown for what it is, because the Day will bring it to light. It will be revealed with fire, and the fire will test the quality of each man's work. If what he has built survives, he will receive his reward. If it is burned up, he will suffer

[10]Both the rich man and the beggar are depicted as being conscious in their new states beyond the grave.

[11]The thief on the cross is promised immediate fellowship with Christ. In the light of Lk 16:22–23, this is evidently a conscious relationship. Paul speaks of being caught up into paradise in 2Co 12:4 (*eis ton paradeison*). The same word is used in Rev.

loss; he himself will be saved, but only as one escaping through the flames.[12]

2Co 5:6–8 Therefore we are always confident and know that as long as we are at home in the body we are away from the Lord. We live by faith, not by sight. We are confident, I say, and would prefer to be away from the body and at home with the Lord.[13]

Php 1:21,23–24 For to me, to live is Christ and to die is gain. . . . I am torn between the two: I desire to depart and be with Christ, which is better by far; but it is more necessary for you that I remain in the body.[14]

1Th 4:14 We believe that Jesus died and rose again and so we believe that God will bring with Jesus those who have fallen asleep in him.[15]

Rev 6:9–10 When he opened the fifth seal, I saw under the altar the souls of those who had been slain because of the word of God and the testimony they had maintained. They called out in a loud voice, "How long, Sovereign Lord, holy and true, until you judge the inhabitants of the earth and avenge our blood?"[16]

Rev 14:13 Then I heard a voice from heaven say, "Write: Blessed are the dead who die in the Lord from now on." "Yes," says the Spirit, "they will rest from their labour, for their deeds will follow them."[17]

2:7: "To him who overcomes, I will give the right to eat from the tree of life, which is in the paradise of God." The term "paradise" is evidently a synonym for heaven.

[12]The reference to fire has been referred to the fires of purgatory. This is an untenable interpretation, because (a) the term "Day" in v. 13 refers to the day of Christ's return (cf. 1:8, "the day of our Lord Jesus Christ"), not the intermediate state between death and the final resurrection, occurring at Christ's return; (b) the judgment in question is not focused on the individual *persons,* but on their *work* relative to the church: "the fire will test the quality of each man's *work*" (v. 14).

[13]Paul states the alternatives: to be away from the body is to be at home with the Lord. That the latter is preferable for the apostle implies that he understood this in terms of conscious fellowship with Christ.

[14]Given the intense spiritual relationship with Christ that the apostle enjoyed during life, his statement that it would be *better by far* to die and be with Christ certainly implies the expectation of *conscious* fellowship.

[15]On the metaphorical language of sleep, see note 9 above. In 5:6, Paul uses "sleep" in yet another metaphorical sense, i.e., spiritual drowsiness and complacency.

[16]The souls of the martyrs under the altar, clearly conscious, call out for God's justice.

[17]The Christian dead enjoy rest from the labour and conflict of their earthly pilgrimage.

FOR FURTHER READING

See books listed on page 138.

12

GENERAL ESCHATOLOGY

General eschatology deals with those events that are to occur at the close of human history. Topics discussed here include the second coming of Christ, the Rapture, the Millenium, the general resurrection, the final judgment, and the eternal state.

"Lo! He comes, He comes to reign; we may try to build His throne, but we shall not accomplish it. But when He comes, He shall build His throne Himself on solid pillars of light and sit and judge in Jerusalem amidst His saints, gloriously" (Charles H. Spurgeon, Sermon, "Looking Unto Jesus").

The Second Coming of Christ

Mt 24:36–39 "No one knows about that day or hour, not even the angels in heaven, nor the Son, but only the Father. As it was in the days of Noah, so it will be at the coming of the Son of Man. For in the days before the flood, people were eating and drinking, marrying and giving in marriage, up to the day Noah entered the ark; and they knew nothing about what would happen until the flood came and took them all away. That is how it will be at the coming of the Son of Man."[1]

Mt 24:42,44 "Therefore keep watch, because you do not know on what day your Lord will come. . . . So you also must be ready, because the Son of Man will come at an hour when you do not expect him."

Mt 25:31–32 "When the Son of Man comes

[1]All attempts to set dates for the Second Coming are contrary to the clear teachings of Christ. The sudden return of Christ will mean judgment for a world caught up in dissipation and the cares of life.

in his glory, and all the angels with him, he will sit on his throne in heavenly glory. All the nations will be gathered before him, and he will separate the people one from another as a shepherd separates the sheep from the goats."[2]

Lk 21:25,27 "There will be signs in the sun, moon and stars. On the earth, nations will be in anguish and perplexity at the roaring and tossing of the sea. . . . At that time they will see the Son of Man coming in a cloud with power and great glory."[3]

Lk 21:34–35 "Be careful, or your hearts will be weighed down with dissipation, drunkenness and the anxieties of life, and that day will close on you unexpectedly like a trap. For it will come upon all those who live on the face of the whole earth."[4]

Ac 1:10–11 They were looking intently up into the sky as he was going, when suddenly two men dressed in white stood beside them. "Men of Galilee," they said, "why do you stand here looking into the sky? This same Jesus, who has been taken from you into heaven, will come back in the same way you have seen him go into heaven."[5]

1Co 4:5 Therefore judge nothing before the appointed time; wait till the Lord comes. He will bring to light what is hidden in darkness and will expose the motives of men's hearts. At that time each will receive his praise from God.

Php 3:20 But our citizenship is in heaven. And we eagerly await a Saviour from there, the Lord Jesus Christ. . . .

Col 3:4 When Christ, who is your life, appears, then you also will appear with him in glory.

1Th 4:15–17 According to the Lord's own word, we tell you that we who are still alive, who are left till the coming of the Lord, will certainly not precede those who have fallen asleep. For the Lord himself will come down from heaven, with a loud command, with the voice of the archangel and with the

[2]Christ came first in the form of a servant; he will return as the Judge of all mankind.

[3]The coming of Christ will be immediately preceded by a period of cosmic and terrestrial distress. Some interpreters have referred this language to a coming of Christ in judgment upon Jerusalem in A.D. 70, in light of the statement concerning "this generation" in v.32.

[4]Believers are warned to be watchful. The Second Coming is not an event of merely local significance, but will affect the entire world.

[5]Both the Ascension and the Second Coming involve the physical and personal presence of Jesus Christ. The New Testament does not teach a purely "spiritual" return of Christ through the Holy Spirit or in the spread of his teachings, as some scholars have suggested.

trumpet call of God, and the dead in Christ will rise first. After that, we who are still alive and are left will be caught up with them in the clouds to meet the Lord in the air. And so we will be with the Lord forever.[6]

1Th 5:1–3 Now, brothers, about times and dates we do not need to write to you, for you know very well that the day of the Lord will come like a thief in the night. While people are saying, "Peace and safety," destruction will come on them suddenly, as labour pains on a pregnant woman, and they will not escape.[7]

2Th 2:1–4,8 Concerning the coming of our Lord Jesus Christ and our being gathered to him, we ask you, brothers, not to become easily unsettled or alarmed by some prophecy, report or letter supposed to have come from us, saying that the day of the Lord has already come. Don't let anyone deceive you in any way, for [that day will not come] until the rebellion occurs and the man of lawlessness is revealed, the man doomed to destruction. He opposes and exalts himself over everything that is called God or is worshipped, and even sets himself up in God's temple, proclaiming himself to be God. . . . The lawless one will be revealed, whom the Lord Jesus will overthrow with the breath of his mouth and destroy by the splendour of his coming.[8]

2Ti 4:8 Now there is in store for me the crown of righteousness, which the Lord, the righteous Judge, will award to me on that day—and not only to me, but also to all who have longed for his appearing.

Tit 2:13 . . . while we wait for the blessed hope—the glorious appearing of our great God and Saviour, Jesus Christ.[9]

Heb 9:28 So Christ was sacrificed once to take away the sins of many people; and he will appear a second time, not to bear sin, but to bring salvation to those who are waiting for him.

Jas 5:7–8 Be patient, then, brothers, until

[6]Paul describes the rapture of the church at the time of the second advent.

[7]Christ's return will bring a judgment upon the world that is sudden, unexpected, and inescapable.

[8]The Antichrist figure is to arise prior to the Second Coming. He will be decisively overthrown by Christ's advent.

[9]This text teaches the deity of Jesus Christ: he is the *great God* and Saviour (*tou megalou Theou kai sōtēros*).

the Lord's coming. See how the farmer waits for the land to yield its valuable crop and how patient he is for the autumn and spring rains. You too, be patient and stand firm, because the Lord's coming is near.

2Pe 3:3–4, 8–10 First of all, you must understand that in the last days scoffers will come, scoffing and following their own evil desires. They will say, "Where is this 'coming' he promised? Ever since our fathers died, everything goes on as it has since the beginning of creation." . . . But do not forget this one thing, dear friends: With the Lord a day is like a thousand years, and a thousand years like a day.[10] The Lord is not slow in keeping his promise, as some understand slowness. He is patient with you, not wanting anyone to perish, but everyone to come to repentance. But the day of the Lord will come like a thief. The heavens will disappear with a roar; the elements will be destroyed by fire, and the earth and everything in it will be laid bare.

[10]Cf. Ps 90:4, "For a thousand years in thy sight are but as yesterday when it is past, or as a watch in the night."

1Jn 2:28 And now, dear children, continue in him, so that when he appears we may be confident and unashamed before him at his coming.

1Jn 3:2–3 Dear friends, now we are children of God, and what we will be has not yet been made known. But we know that when he appears, we shall be like him, for we shall see him as he is. Everyone who has this hope in him purifies himself, just as he is pure.[11]

[11]In the New Testament, the Second Coming is not a topic for speculation, but an incentive for obedient and holy living.

Rev 16:15 "Behold, I come like a thief! Blessed is he who stays awake and keeps his clothes with him, so that he may not go naked and be shamefully exposed."

Rev 22:20 He who testifies to these things says, "Yes, I am coming soon."

Millennial Views

The term "millennium" derives from the reference to the thousand-year reign of Christ with the saints in Rev 20:4–6. The various millennial views reflect different understandings of the nature of this period (literal vs. symbolic), and different understandings of the chronological relationship of the second coming of Christ to the millennial period, the Great Tribulation, and other events of the last days.

PREMILLENNIAL, PRETRIBULATIONAL (DISPENSATIONAL)

According to this view, Christ returns *prior* to the Millennium ("premill"), understood as a literal thousand-year period, and prior to the seven-year period known as the Great Tribulation ("pretrib"). Christ first comes secretly *for* the church (the Rapture), and then publicly *with* the church to institute the millennial kingdom; the church does not go through the Great Tribulation.

Mt 24:3,21,29–30 As Jesus was sitting on the Mount of Olives, the disciples came to him privately. "Tell us," they said, "when will this [destruction of Temple, vv. 1–2] happen, and what will be the sign of your coming and of the end of the age?". ". . . For then there will be great distress, unequalled from the beginning of the world until now—and never to be equalled again. . . . Immediately after the distress of those days. . . . the sign of the Son of Man will appear in the sky, and all the nations of the earth will mourn. They will see the Son of Man coming on the clouds of the sky, with power and great glory."[12]

Mt 24:37,40–41 "As it was in the days of Noah, so it will be at the coming of the Son of Man. . . . Two men will be in the field; one will be taken and the other left. Two women will be grinding with a hand mill; one will be taken and the other left."

1Th 4:15–17 According to the Lord's own word, we tell you that we who are still alive, who are left till the coming of the Lord, will certainly not precede those who have fallen asleep. For the Lord himself will come down

[12]Christ returns publicly (with the church) after the period of the Great Tribulation to institute the millennial kingdom (Rev 20:4–6). On the Great Tribulation, see also Rev 7:14, 11:2. This period of ununequalled tribulation is also identified with the seventieth prophetic week (1 day=1 year) of Da 9:27).

[13]In the premill, pretrib (dispensational) view, Mt 24:37,40–41; 1Th 4:15–17; Rev 3:10 refer to the secret coming of Christ for the church (Rapture) immediately prior to the Great Tribulation. Some recent dispensationalists would not see Mt 24:37,

from heaven, with a loud command, with the voice of the archangel and with the trumpet call of God, and the dead in Christ will rise first. After that, we who are still alive and are left will be caught up with them in the clouds to meet the Lord in the air. And so we will be with the Lord forever.

Rev 3:10 [to the church in Philadelphia]: "Since you have kept my command to endure patiently, I will also keep you from the hour of trial that is going to come upon the whole world to test those who live on the earth."[13]

Rev 20:4–6 I saw thrones on which were seated those who had been given authority to judge. And I saw the souls of those who had been beheaded because of their testimony for Jesus and because of the word of God. They had not worshipped the beast or his image and had not received his mark on their foreheads or their hands. They came to life and reigned with Christ a thousand years. (The rest of the dead did not come to life until the thousand years were ended.) This is the first resurrection. Blessed and holy are those who have part in the first resurrection. The second death has no power over them, but they will be priests of God and of Christ and will reign with him for a thousand years.[14]

Rev 21:1,3–4 Then I saw a new heaven and a new earth, for the first heaven and the first earth had passed away. . . . And I heard a loud voice from the throne saying, "Now the dwelling of God is with men. . . . There will be no more death or mourning or crying or pain, for the old order of things has passed away."[15]

PREMILLENNIAL, POSTTRIBULATIONAL (NON-DISPENSATIONAL)

According to this view, Christ returns *prior* to the millennium ("premill"), understood as a literal thousand-year period, but *after* the Great Tribulation ("post-trib"). According to this view,

40–41 as a reference to the Rapture.

[14]A literal thousand-year reign of Christ and the saints on earth; both the first and second resurrections are literal resurrections.

[15]A description of the eternal state (see also Isa 65:17; 66:22). During the millennial period evil and conflict are still present; in the eternal state, Christ and the Father have completely defeated all the powers of evil and death itself.

[16]In the premill, posttribulational ("pre-post") view, refers to the public coming of Christ after the Tribulation.

[17]Refers to the posttribulational public rapture of the church at the coming of Christ.

[18]Understood as referring specifically to the church of Philadelphia in its unique situation, or more generally, to God's assurance of grace to believers *in the midst of* tribulation. Those who hold to the "pre-post" view point to texts such as Jn 17:15 to argue that the church will go through the Tribulation: "My prayer is not that you take them out of the world but that you protect them from the evil one."

[19]Christ's return after the Great Tribulation.

[20]Christ returns to institute a thousand-year reign on earth with the saints; both the first and the second resurrections are literal.

[21]As in the dispensational view, understood to refer to the eternal state.

[22]Christ returns after the Tribulation; the church goes through this time of distress.

there is no *secret* rapture of the church; the church does go through the Tribulation.

Mt 24:3, 21, 29–30[19] (see above for text)

Mt 24:37, 40–41[16] (see above for text)

1Th 4:15–17[17] (see above for text)

Rev 3:10[18] (see above for text)

Rev 20:4–6[20] (see above for text)

Rev 21:1,3–4[21] (see above for text)

AMILLENNIAL

According to this view, there is no literal thousand-year reign of Christ with the saints on earth. The return of Christ is followed immediately by the general resurrection of both the righteous and the wicked, the Last Judgment, and the passage into the eternal state.

1Th 4:15–17[23] (see above for text)

Jn 5:28–29 "Do not be amazed at this, for a time is coming when all who are in their graves will hear his [Christ's] voice and come out—those who have done good will rise to live, and those who have done evil will rise to be condemned."[24]

Rev 20:4–6[25] (see above for text)

Mt 25:31–32 "When the Son of Man comes in his glory, and all the angels with him, he will sit on his throne in heavenly glory. All the nations will be gathered before him, and he will separate the people one from another as a shepherd separates the sheep from the goats."[26]

Rev 21:1,3–4[27] (see above for text)

POSTMILLENNIAL

According to this view, Christ returns *after* ("post") a long period of expansion and spiritual prosperity for the church, caused by the Spirit's blessing of the preaching of the gospel. The "millennium" is not a literal thousand years, but

[23]At the return of Christ, the living believers are raptured to meet the returning Lord after the Christian dead have first been raised.

[24]A simultaneous resurrection of both righteous and wicked at the coming of Christ.

[25]In the amillennial view, the thousand years are taken to be symbolic of the entire church age; the first resurrection is taken to be spiritual, referring either to the believer's regeneration, or to a spiritual reign of the Christian with Christ after death during the intermediate state. The second resurrection is literal. Texts such as Jn 5:25 ("I tell you the truth, a time is coming and has now come when the dead will hear the voice of the Son of God and those who hear will live") and Eph 2:6 ("And God raised us up with Christ and seated us with him in the heavenly realms in Christ Jesus") are cited in support of a spiritual resurrection. Premillennialists, however, argue that both resurrections are literal, inasmuch as the same Greek word *(ezēsan,* they lived) is used of both resurrections in 20:4 and 20:5.

[26]The Last Judgment follows immediately upon the return of Christ. In the non-dispensational premillennial view, the Judgment occurs at the end of the millennium, prior to the passage to the eternal state. In the dispensational view, this text refers to a judgment of all Gentiles then living at the return of Christ after the Tribulation and at the beginning of the millennium. The judgment of the wicked (deceased) occurs at the end of the millennium.

[27]The eternal state.

this extended period of spiritual prosperity prior to Christ's return.

Isa 2:2,4 In the last days the mountain of the Lord's temple will be established as chief among the mountains; it will be raised above the hills, and all nations will stream to it. . . . He will judge between the nations and will settle disputes for many peoples. They will beat their swords into ploughshares and their spears into pruning hooks. . . .[28]

[28]In the postmill view, the "temple" is taken to refer to the church; the "last days" are the latter days of the church *age,* prior to Christ's return.

Da 2:31,34–35 "You looked, O king [Nebuchadnezzar], and there before you stood a large statue—an enormous, dazzling statue, awesome in appearance. . . . While you were watching, a rock was cut out, but not by human hands. It struck the statue on its feet of iron and clay and smashed them. Then the iron, the clay, the bronze, the silver and the gold were broken to pieces. . . . The wind swept them away without leaving a trace. But the rock that struck the statue became a huge mountain and filled the whole earth."[29]

[29]Daniel interprets Nebuchadnezzar's dream. The "rock" is the kingdom of Jesus Christ which overcomes the world's empires and expands throughout the earth.

Mt 13:31–32 He told them another parable: "The kingdom of heaven is like a mustard seed, which a man took and planted in his field. Though it is the smallest of all your seeds, yet when it grows, it is the largest of garden plants and becomes a tree, so that the birds of the air come and perch in its branches."[30]

[30]The dramatic growth of the kingdom from rather insignificant beginnings.

Mt 13:33 He told them still another parable: "The kingdom of heaven is like yeast that a woman took and mixed into a large amount of flour until it worked all through the dough."[31]

[31]An illustration of the *pervasive* impact of the kingdom of Christ.

1Co 15:22–26 For as in Adam all die, so in Christ all will be made alive. But each in his own turn: Christ, the first fruits; then, when he comes, those who belong to him. Then the end will come, when he hands over the kingdom of God the Father after he has destroyed all dominion, authority and power. For he must reign until he has put all his enemies under his feet. The last enemy to be destroyed is death.[32]

[32]In the postmill view, death, the *last* enemy, is destroyed at the second coming, and this destruction is manifested by the resurrection. *Prior* to this, while Christ is still reigning at the right hand of the Father, the hostile spiritual powers and authorities are progressively subdued.

Rev 20:4–6[33] (see above for text)

Rev 20:7–9 When the thousand years are over, Satan will be released from his prison and will go out to deceive the nations in the four corners of the earth—Gog and Magog —to gather them for battle. . . . They . . . surrounded the camp of God's people. . . . But fire came down from heaven and devoured them.[34]

The General Resurrection

Job 19:25–27 "I know that my Redeemer lives, and that in the end he will stand upon the earth. And after my skin has been destroyed, yet in my flesh I will see God; I myself will see him with my own eyes— I, and not another."

Isa 26:19 But your dead will live; their bodies will rise. You who dwell in the dust, wake up and shout for joy. Your dew is like the dew of the morning: the earth will give birth to her dead.

Da 12:2 "Multitudes who sleep in the dust of the earth will awake: some to everlasting life, others to shame and everlasting contempt."[35]

Mt 22:29–32 Jesus replied, "You are in error because you do not know the Scriptures or the power of God. At the resurrection people will neither marry nor be given in marriage; they will be like the angels in heaven. But about the resurrection of the dead—have you not read what God said to you, 'I am the God of Abraham, the God of Isaac, and the God of Jacob'? He is not the God of the dead but of the living."[36]

Lk 20:37 "But in the account of the bush, even Moses showed that the dead rise, for he calls the Lord 'the God of Abraham, and the God of Isaac, and the God of Jacob.' "

Jn 5:28–29 "Do not be amazed at this, for a time is coming when all who are in their graves will hear his voice and come out— those who have done good will rise to live,

[33]The first resurrection is spiritual, taken to refer to regeneration, or to the intermediate state after death, or to the "resurrection" and vindication of the Christian faith for which the martyrs died.

[34]At the end of the millennial period, there will be a period of general apostasy and tribulation for the people of God. The enemies of the people of God ("Gog and Magog") will be vanquished, however, by the returning Christ. On fire from heaven, cf. 2Th 1:7, "when the Lord Jesus is revealed from heaven in blazing fire with his powerful angels."

[35]This is perhaps the most explicit OT text on the general resurrection. The doctrine of the resurrection was only fully revealed after the resurrection of Jesus Christ.

[36]In debate with the Sadducees, Christ teaches the resurrection of the dead by citing Ex 3:6, the passage concerning the burning bush. Abraham, Isaac, and Jacob live before God, and will share in the general resurrection.

and those who have done evil will rise to be condemned."

Jn 6:39–40 "And this is the will of him who sent me, that I shall lose none of all that he has given me, but raise them up at the last day. For my Father's will is that everyone who looks to the Son, and believes in him shall have eternal life, and I will raise him up at the last day."

Jn 11:25-26 Jesus said to her [Martha], "I am the resurrection and the life. He who believes in me will live, even though he dies; and whoever lives and believes in me will never die."[37]

[37]That is, will never die.

Ac 24:15 "And I [Paul] have the same hope in God as these men, that there will be a resurrection of both the righteous and the wicked."[38]

[38]Paul is on trial before Felix in Caesarea.

Ro 6:5 If we have been united with him in his death, we will certainly also be united with him in his resurrection.

Ro 8:11 If the Spirit of him who raised Jesus from the dead is living in you, he who raised Christ from the dead will also give life to your mortal bodies through his Spirit, who lives in you.

Ro 8:23 Not only so, but we ourselves, who have the firstfruits of the Spirit, groan inwardly as we wait eagerly for our adoption as sons, the redemption of our bodies.[39]

[39]The redemption of the body occurs at the resurrection.

1Co 15:20–23; 51–52 But Christ has indeed been raised from the dead, the first-fruits of those who have fallen asleep. For since death came through a man, the resurrection of the dead comes also through a man. For as in Adam all die, so in Christ all will be made alive. But each in his own turn: Christ, the firstfruits; then, when he comes, those who belong to him. . . . Listen, I tell you a mystery: We will not all sleep, but we will all be changed—in a flash, in the twinkling of an eye, at the last trumpet. For the trumpet will sound, the dead will be raised imperishable, and we will be changed.[40]

[40]Vv. 12–58 in chapter 15 are devoted to this topic and constitute the most extensive discussion in the NT concerning the resurrection.

Php 3:10–11 I want to know Christ and the power of his resurrection and the fellowship of sharing in his sufferings, becoming like him in his death, and so, somehow, to attain to the resurrection from the dead.

1Th 4:16–17 For the Lord himself will come down from heaven, with a loud command, with the voice of the archangel and with the trumpet call of God, and the dead in Christ will rise first. After that, we who are still alive and are left will be caught up with them in the clouds to meet the Lord in the air. And so we will be with the Lord forever.

Rev 20:4–6 I saw thrones on which were seated those who had been given authority to judge. And I saw the souls of those who had been beheaded because of their testimony for Jesus and because of the word of God. They had not worshipped the beast or his image and had not received his mark on their foreheads or their hands. They came to life and reigned with Christ a thousand years. (The rest of the dead did not come to life until the thousand years were ended.) This is the first resurrection. Blessed and holy are those who have part in the first resurrection. The second death has no power over them, but they will be priests of God and of Christ and will reign with him for a thousand years.[41]

[41]For the various interpretations of this passage, see the discussions in Chapter 12, Millennial Views.

The Final Judgment

Ps 96:13 They will sing before the Lord, for he comes, he comes to judge the earth. He will judge the world in righteousness and the peoples in his truth.

Ecc 12:14 For God will bring every deed into judgment, including every hidden thing, whether it is good or evil.

Mt 12:36–37 "But I tell you that men will have to give account on the day of judgment for every careless word they have spoken. For by your words you will be acquitted, and by your words you will be condemned."

Mt 13:39–42 "The harvest is the end of the

age, and the harvesters are angels. As the weeds are pulled up and burned in the fire, so it will be at the end of the age. The Son of Man will send out his angels, and they will weed out of his kingdom everything that causes sin and all who do evil. They will throw them into the fiery furnace, where there will be weeping and gnashing of teeth."[42]

[42]Christ explains the parable of the wheat and the tares.

Mt 13:47–50 "Once again, the kingdom of heaven is like a net that was let down into the lake and caught all kinds of fish. When it was full, the fishermen pulled it up on the shore. Then they sat down and collected the good fish in baskets, but threw the bad way. This is how it will be at the end of the age. The angels will come and separate the wicked from the righteous and throw them into the fiery furnace, where there will be weeping and gnashing of teeth."

Mt 25:32–33,46 "All the nations will be gathered before him, and he will separate the people one from another as a shepherd separates the sheep from the goats. He will put the sheep on his right and the goats on his left. . . . Then they will go away to eternal punishment, but the righteous to eternal life."

Lk 11:31–32 "The Queen of the South [of Sheba] will rise at the judgment with the men of this generation and condemn them, for she came from the ends of the earth to listen to Solomon's wisdom, and now one greater than Solomon is here. The men of Nineveh will stand up at the judgment with this generation and condemn it, for they repented at the preaching of Jonah, and now one greater than Jonah is here."[43]

[43]Jesus rebukes those Jews of his own generation for their unbelief.

Jn 12:47–48 "As for the person who hears my words but does not keep them, I do not judge him. For I did not come to judge the world, but to save it.[44] There is a judge for the one who rejects me and does not accept my words; that very word which I spoke will condemn him at the last day."

[44]In his first advent Jesus came as Saviour; in his second advent, he will return as the Judge of all mankind.

Ac 17:31 "For he [God] has set a day when

he will judge the world with justice by the man he has appointed. He has given proof of this to all men by raising him from the dead."[45]

Ro 2:5–8 Because of your stubbornness and your unrepentant heart, you are storing up wrath against yourself for the day of God's wrath, when his righteous judgment will be revealed. God "will give to each person according to what he has done." To those who by persisting in doing good seek glory, honour and immortality, he will give eternal life. But for those who are self-seeking and who reject the truth and follow evil, there will be wrath and anger.[46]

Ro 14:11–12 It is written: " 'As surely as I live,' says the Lord, 'Every knee will bow before me; every tongue will confess to God.' " So then, each of us will give an account of himself to God.[47]

1Co 3:12–13 If any man builds on this foundation using gold, silver, costly stones, wood, hay or straw, his work will be shown for what it is, because the Day [of Judgment] will bring it to light. It will be revealed with fire, and the fire will test the quality of each man's work.

**2Co 5:10* For we must all appear before the judgment seat of Christ, that each one may receive what is due to him for the things done while in the body, whether good or bad.

Heb 9:27 Man is destined to die once, and after that to face judgment.[48]

Heb 10:26–27 If we deliberately keep on sinning after we have received the knowledge of the truth, no sacrifice for sins is left, but only a fearful expectation of judgment and of raging fire that will consume the enemies of God.

2Pe 2:9 If this is so, then the Lord knows how to rescue godly men from trials and to hold the unrighteous for the day of judgment, while continuing their punishment.

[45]The conclusion of Paul's speech at the Areopagus in Athens.

[46]Paul is not here teaching salvation by good works; this he explicitly excludes in Ro 3:28. Rather, genuine good works are a sign that the grace of God is active in the heart.

[47]The immediate context is that of not passing judgment on a weaker brother in matters of food. The concept of a final judgment is the ultimate foundation for moral accountability and personal responsibility in human affairs.

[48]This text shows clearly that the NT view of the afterlife is incompatible with Eastern doctrines of karma and reincarnation.

2Pe 3:7 By the same word the present heavens and earth are reserved for fire, being kept for the day of judgment and destruction of ungodly men.

Jude 6 And the angels who did not keep their positions of authority but abandoned their own home—these he has kept in darkness, bound with everlasting chains for judgment on the great Day.

Rev 6:15–17 Then the kings of the earth, the princes, the generals, the rich, the mighty, and every slave and every free man hid in caves and among the rocks of the mountains. They called to the mountains and the rocks, "Fall on us and hide us from the face of him who sits on the throne and from the wrath of the Lamb! For the great day of their wrath has come, and who can stand?"

Rev 11:18 "The nations were angry; and your wrath has come. The time has come for judging the dead, and for rewarding your servants the prophets and your saints and those who reverence your name, both small and great—and for destroying those who destroy the earth."

Rev 20:12–13 And I saw the dead, great and small, standing before the throne, and books were opened. Another book was opened, which is the book of life. That dead were judged according to what they had done as recorded in the books. The sea gave up the dead that were in it, and death and Hades gave up the dead that were in them, and each person was judged according to what he had done.

The Eternal State

"The last judgment determines, and therefore naturally leads on to, the final state of those who appear before the judgment seat. Their final state is either one of everlasting misery or one of eternal blessedness" (Berkhof).

Da 12:3 "Those who are wise will shine like the brightness of the heavens, and those who lead many to righteousness, like the stars for ever and ever."

Mt 8:11–12 "I say to you that many will come from the east and the west,[49] and will take their places at the feast with Abraham, Isaac and Jacob in the kingdom of heaven. But the subjects of the kingdom will be thrown outside, into the darkness, where there will be weeping and gnashing of teeth."

[49]Jesus' words foreshadow the calling of the Gentiles. The "subjects of the Kingdom" who are cast into the outer darkness are, in this case, unbelieving Israelites.

Mt 13:49–50 "This is how it will be at the end of the age. The angels will come and separate the wicked from the righteous and throw them into the fiery furnace, where there will be weeping and gnashing of teeth."

Mt 18:8–9 "If your hand or foot causes you to sin, cut it off and throw it away. It is better for you to enter life maimed or crippled than to have two hands or two feet and be thrown into eternal fire. And if your eye causes you to sin, gouge it out and throw it away. It is better for you to enter life with one eye than to have two eyes and be thrown into the fire of hell."[50]

[50]The graphic language here teaches the enormous gravity in God's sight of persistent sin.

Mt 25:41,46 "Then he will say to those on his left, " 'Depart from me, you who are cursed, into the eternal fire prepared for the devil and his angels. . . .' Then they will go away to eternal punishment, but the righteous to eternal life."

Mk 9:43–48 "If your hand causes you to sin, cut it off. It is better for you to enter life maimed than with two hands to go into hell, where the fire never goes out. And if your foot causes you to sin, cut it off. It is better for you to enter life crippled than to have two feet and be thrown into hell. And if your eye causes you to sin, pluck it out. It is better for you to enter the kingdom of God with one eye than to have two eyes and be thrown into hell, where 'their worm does not die, and the fire is not quenched.' "[51]

[51]Cf. Mt 18:8–9. The Markan text contains a quotation from Isa 66:24.

Lk 16:22–26 "The time came when the beggar died and the angels carried him to Abraham's side. The rich man also died and was buried. In hell, where he was in torment, he looked up and saw Abraham far away, with Lazarus by his side. So he called to him, 'Father Abraham, have pity on me and send Lazarus to dip the tip of his finger in water and cool my tongue, because I am in agony in this fire.' But Abraham replied, 'Son, remember that in your lifetime you received your good things, while Lazarus received bad things, but now he is comforted here and you are in agony. And besides all this, between us and you a great chasm has been fixed, so that those who want to go from here to you cannot, nor can anyone cross over from there to us.' "[52]

[52]"Abraham's side" is a reference to heaven, and may be regarded as the equivalent to "Paradise" in Lk 23:43. The "great chasm" illustrates the finality of one's state after death.

Jn 14:2–3 "In my Father's house are many rooms; if it were not so, I would have told you. I am going there to prepare a place for you. And if I go and prepare a place for you, I will come back and take you to be with me that you also may be where I am."

Ro 8:19–21 The creation waits in eager expectation for the sons of God to be revealed. For the creation was subjected to frustration, not by its own choice, but by the will of the one who subjected it, in hope that the creation itself will be liberated from its bondage to decay and brought into the glorious freedom of the children of God.[53]

[53]In the eternal state, creation itself will be freed from the effects of the Fall and the curse (Ge 3). Compare the statements on the new heavens and the new earth in Rev 21:1; 22:3–5.

2Co 4:17–18 For our light and momentary troubles are achieving for us an eternal glory that far outweighs them all. So we fix our eyes not on what is seen, but on what is unseen. For what is seen is temporary, but what is unseen is eternal.

2Co 5:1 Now we know that if the earthly tent we live in is destroyed, we have a building from God, an eternal house in heaven, not built by human hands.[54]

[54]The "earthly tent" is the present mortal body; the "eternal house" is the resurrection body.

2Th 1:8–9 He will punish those who do not know God and do not obey the gospel of our Lord Jesus. They will be punished with everlasting destruction and shut out from the presence of the Lord and from the majesty of his power. . . .

Heb 12:22–23 But you have come to Mount Zion, to the heavenly Jerusalem, the city of the living God. You have come to thousands upon thousands of angels in joyful assembly, to the church of the firstborn, whose names are written in heaven. You have come to God, the judge of all men, to the spirits of righteous men made perfect. . . .

1Pe 1:3–4 In his great mercy he has given us new birth into a living hope through the resurrection of Jesus Christ from the dead, and into an inheritance that can never perish, spoil or fade—kept in heaven for you.

Jude 7 In a similar way, Sodom and Gomorrah and the surrounding towns gave themselves up to sexual immorality and perversion. They serve as an example of those who suffer the punishment of eternal life.

Rev 14:11 "And the smoke of their torment rises for ever and ever. There is no rest day or night for those who worship the beast and his image, or for anyone who receives the mark of his name."

Rev 20:10,15 And the devil, who deceived them, was thrown into the lake of burning sulphur, where the beast and the false prophet had been thrown. They will be tormented day and night for ever and ever. . . . If anyone's name was not found written in the book of life, he was thrown into the lake of fire.

Rev 21:14 Then I saw a new heaven and a new earth, for the first heaven and the first earth had passed away, and there was no longer any sea. . . . "He will wipe away every tear from their eyes. There will be no more death or mourning or crying or pain, for the old order of things has passed away."

Rev 21:8 "But the cowardly, the unbelieving, the vile, the murderers, the sexually immoral, those who practice magic arts, the idolaters and all liars— their place will be in the fiery lake of burning sulphur. This is the second death."

Rev 22:3–5 No longer will there be any curse. The throne of God and of the Lamb will be in the city, and his servants will serve him. They will see his face and his name will be on their foreheads. There will be no more night. They will not need the light of a lamp or the light of the sun, for the Lord God will give them light. And they will reign for ever and ever.

FOR FURTHER READING

Eschatology

art. "Eschatology" by G. E. Ladd, in *New Bible Dictionary* (1961), pp. 386–391. (A)
BOETTNER, L. *Immortality* (1958), 159pp. (B)
GOULBURN, E. M. *Everlasting punishment* (1880), 191pp. (B)
GUTHRIE, D. *New Testament Theology* (1981), sect. 8, "The future", pp.790–892. (B)
HENDRIKSEN, W. *The Bible on the life hereafter* (1959), 222pp. (A)
MORRIS. L. *The wages of sin: an examination of the New Testament teaching on death* (1955), 28pp. (B)
SALMOND, S. D. F. *The Christian doctrine of immortality* (1895), 703pp. (B)
SHEDD, W. G. T. *Dogmatic Theology* (1888), rep. Vol. II, pp.591–754. (C)
TRAVIS, S. *The Jesus hope* (1974), 128pp. (A)

The Millennium/Tribulation/Rapture/Second Coming

CLOUSE, R. G. *The meaning of the Millennium: four views* (1977), 223pp. (B)
ERICKSON, M. J. *Contemporary options in eschatology: a study of the Millennium* (1977), 197pp. (B)
ALLIS, O. T. *Prophecy and the Church* (1945), 339pp. (Amillennial) (C)
GRIER, W. J. *The momentous event* (1970), 128pp. (Amillennial) (A)
LADD, G. E. *The blessed hope* (1956), 167pp. (Premillennial) (B)
PACHE, R. *The Return of Jesus Christ* (1955), 448pp. (Premillennial) (B)
BOETTNER, L. *The Millennium* (1958), 380pp. (Postmillennial) (B)
MURRAY, I. *The Puritan Hope* (1971), 301pp. (Postmillennial) (B)